Silent Reading

An Introduction to its Study and Teaching

Silent Reading

An Introduction to its Study and Teaching

A. K. PUGH
Faculty of Educational Studies
The Open University

HEINEMANN EDUCATIONAL BOOKS
LONDON

Heinemann Educational Books
LONDON EDINBURGH MELBOURNE AUCKLAND
TORONTO HONG KONG SINGAPORE KUALA LUMPUR
IBADAN NAIROBI JOHANNESBURG
NEW DELHI LUSAKA KINGSTON

ISBN 0 435 10719 4

© A. K. Pugh 1978
First published 1978

Published by
Heinemann Educational Books Ltd
48 Charles Street, London W1X 8AH
Printed and bound in Great Britain by
The Pitman Press, Bath

Contents

Preface

Over a period of several years I have been engaged in teaching and research related to reading in middle, secondary and higher education. This book results from that work. I am particularly indebted to Mr J. Stephenson for first encouraging my interest in this field, Dr Mary H. Neville, with whom I have worked closely on a number of studies, especially those concerned with the development of reading fluency, and to Mr A. Laing and Professor K. Lovell who supervised my higher degree researches at the University of Leeds.

Although this book is newly written, parts of it draw upon my M.Phil. thesis, while the material for some other sections has appeared in various journal articles and conference papers. Full bibliographical references are given at the end of the text.

I have benefited from numerous discussions with fellow researchers and with my students, but I am especially grateful to those colleagues and friends who have read and commented on all or part of the manuscript at some stage during the writing. For this, thanks are due to Dr L. J. Chapman, Pam Czerniewska, Dr J. L. Dobson, Dr Mary H. Neville, N. J. Small, Alan Stokes and Peter Whalley. I also wish to acknowledge the advice and information on reading in French-speaking countries which Professor Jean Burion has kindly given. Naturally, any defects which may remain in the text are my responsibility.

Finally, I must thank Mrs Margaret Greaves and Mrs Hilda Short who shared the typing of the manuscript.

A. K. PUGH

Introduction

Silent reading is an important activity in adult life, and one which has received a fair amount of attention from psychological and other researchers during this century. Yet, on the whole, schools have paid little attention to the development of silent reading ability. This book argues that it is both possible and desirable to help children to learn how to read beyond the early stages, which have so far received most attention. The difficulties of teaching silent reading are fully examined since only by overcoming them and the problems involved in observing and assessing this kind of reading behaviour, will teaching methods be developed and refined. My concern, however, is less with those technical issues in areas such as measurement which are of interest in their own right, but rather with providing information and interpretations which will help those who wish to teach silent reading.

What precisely is meant by 'silent reading' emerges as the book proceeds, but Chapters 3 and 5 are especially relevant to clarifying my use of the term. However, the book is written in such a way that, although topics inevitably overlap, the chapters may be read separately and in almost any order, since on more important issues the cross references to other chapters are normally given in the text. At this point it might be helpful to explain the structure of the book.

Of the eight chapters, the first six are principally concerned with the teaching of silent reading and the last two with its study. In Chapter 1 there is a broad look at the effect of neglecting the teaching of reading in secondary and higher education, some evidence of the neglect, and an attempt to account for it. The second chapter uses an historical perspective to examine the study and teaching of silent reading up to about the Second World War. The third chapter is especially concerned with the child's beginning silent reading, and with reading fluency. Some practical approaches are reviewed and a developmental framework is suggested. Chapters 4 and 5 review courses used with adults and with students in higher education with a view to developing speed or efficiency in reading, especially reading for study purposes. The main argument here is that there is a danger of unduly circumscribing what is to be taught simply because some reading tasks appear to lend themselves more readily than others to testing. Chapter 6 asks what should be taught in schools, by whom, and using what methods. Some suggestions are made about how the teaching might be done, but the question of whose responsibility it is remains a vexed one.

The final chapters, 7 and 8, are rather more technical and are concerned with concepts such as comprehension, readability, and reading interests, as well as with methods for testing and studying silent reading behaviour. However, the technical matters have considerable relevance since, as has already been suggested, the teaching of silent reading has suffered from the elusive nature of the skilled behaviour to be taught. Furthermore, the way in which concepts related to the teaching of reading are defined has considerable effect on what is taught. The danger is that certain concepts may grow divorced from reality, and transfer of learning from school tasks to real situations will then be unlikely.

In view of the relative lack of interest in silent reading, there is little experience of practical teaching of silent reading in schools to draw upon. Consequently, this book has often to be content to raise issues without being able to supply prescriptions, and at times may appear to raise considerably more questions than it answers. A number of fairly well established theories and practices are found not to stand up to close scrutiny, especially when one tries to take into account the needs of students and children in realistic reading situations. At the risk of undermining what established practice there is, it has seemed important in searching for sound bases for the development of effective silent reading, to question as well as to make suggestions, and to draw attention to areas of difficulty rather than attempt to ignore them.

I

The Cause for Concern about Silent Reading

The extent of adult illiteracy, the standard of reading achieved by schoolchildren and, consequently, the teaching of reading in schools, have aroused considerable interest and concern during the past few years. Estimates such as that of Haviland (1973)* of a possible 2 million adult illiterates, often accepted without the estimator's cautions as to how the figure is derived, led to special Government financial support for adult literacy schemes. The publication of the National Foundation for Educational Research's latest survey of school reading standards (Start and Wells, 1972), and the ensuing debate, led to the setting up of the Committee of Enquiry under the Chairmanship of Sir Alan Bullock which reported on the teaching of English, and especially of reading, in schools (DES 1975). Unfortunately, through lack of funds, the many and extensive recommendations of that report have been tested in practice far less than they deserve.

At least since the findings of Joyce Morris (Morris, 1966) concern about standards has often focussed attention on the inadequate preparation of infant and primary teachers for teaching reading. The Bullock report has, among other things, given rise to considerable debate about the measuring instruments used for monitoring standards and about the desirability of regular national monitoring of reading ability in schools. In all this, some extremely important areas have been almost entirely missed, for the emphasis in the teaching of reading is still largely on initial and remedial teaching. For example, although it shows awareness of the need for the development of reading skills beyond the primary school, the Bullock report offers little practical help to the secondary schoolteacher, nor does it provide him with much of a theoretical basis for devising his own

* See the section *References*, toward the end of the book for full details of this and all publications referred to in the text.

practices. The debates about testing have also done little to clarify what behaviours should be developed and tested at this level. Thus it appears from their report (especially pp. 16–17) that Start and Wells are somewhat concerned about the vagueness of what is being tested in the national surveys, although Davies (1977) argues that the tests are suitable for their purpose.

An important theme in this book is that silent reading has for various historical and practical reasons been largely neglected as an activity in which children and adults need help and can be given it. On the face of it, this seems a strange omission since silent reading is the normal mode of reading for most literate adults. The omission is also, in many ways, as disturbing as the better publicized lack of constructive attention to problems of basic illiteracy in children and adults. As many commentators have pointed out, literacy is not an absolute level of attainment but is relative to what one wants or needs to do in reading and writing. What has come to be known as functional illiteracy may be more widespread than is suspected.

Standards of reading beyond school

The effects of neglecting the development of silent reading in secondary education might, if the evidence were available, be best judged by examining the functional reading performance of people who have finished their schooling. There have been some attempts to assess functional literacy, notably by Murphy (1975) who reports a national survey of the daily reading habits of 5,073 adults in the United States together with results of functional reading tests for about 8,000 people. Delineation of the reading skills required in jobs is being undertaken in Canada as part of a larger programme of research into occupational skills, and Smith (1976) produces useful information from this study on what needs to be read, and by whom for their work. As Bormuth (1973) notes, there are considerable problems in defining literacy among adults and when looking at functional literacy it is necessary to define clearly what needs to be read in order to assess how well a person is likely to be able to cope with the reading demands of his job.

Unfortunately, there is little evidence in Britain about the reading abilities of adults. The estimated number of adult illiterates in Britain is open to question and, in order to obtain evidence on illiteracy, considerably more work needs to be done along the lines of the North American researches referred to above. There is also very little written about the reading performance of students in further education. One study in this area (Gardner, 1966) points to a dissatisfaction with students' reading attainment but, although a fairly large sample was used, the tests employed do not appear to have been entirely suitable.

For lack of evidence elsewhere, it seems useful to look at the reading standards of those students who have succeeded in the educational system, at least to the extent that they have entered a university. Since British universities are very selective institutions, which students can only enter after successfully completing numerous examinations which require fairly high levels of literacy, one might expect that there would be little need of further help with reading at this level. However, the very fact that courses of the speed reading type appear to be in fairly heavy demand may, as Beard (1972, pp. 185*ff*) suggests, be taken as evidence of the fact that students do feel a need to obtain advice on how to read and how to study.

Precise empirical evidence on the reading standards and difficulties of university undergraduates is not available, but a number of studies do suggest that there are grounds for disquiet. Reid (1973) interviewed a small sample of students at Edinburgh University who were concerned about their studies and found that their difficulties particularly related to reading. Beard (1972, pp. 188-190) found that many of her postgraduate students of education did not read quickly or skim, and that they showed little awareness of the value of an index in a book. Mann (1973) carried out a questionnaire survey on the use of books at Sheffield University and concluded (p. 14) that the students were, on the whole, uninstructed in the use of books and that lecturers could do more than they do at present to improve the situation. Latham (1975) mentions a questionnaire survey which he carried out in 1967 among lecturers teaching medical and dental students at London University. In the opinion of the majority of their lecturers most students were 'illiterate', presumably in the functional sense already referred to, and had particular problems because, according to their lecturers, they tended to read slowly, could not select the essential from the inessential or make usable notes.

A few British universities, and a larger number of other institutions of higher education, have shown awareness of these problems by offering courses for students. Apart from a course at Sussex (Watts 1969, 1972) which was given by a commercial organization specializing in courses in reading skills, only two British universities have offered courses over a sustained period. These are Brunel (Thomas, and Harri-Augstein, 1976) and Leeds. The course at Leeds is referred to more fully later but it is worth mentioning here that there appeared to be a demand among students for help. About one in ten of all new native English-speaking students applied for a place on a course designed to help them read more effectively for study purposes. Of these a substantial number actually completed the course which was entirely voluntary and was, of necessity, held at inconvenient times. Although the evidence on reading standards in universities is not precise and must be viewed with caution, there are grounds for thinking that students do not read as well as they themselves would like to or as their tutors wish and expect them to do.

Possible causes of functional illiteracy in adults

Various explanations have been offered as to why intelligent adults do not read as well as they might. A survey of adults in a small town in the United States (Gray and Rogers, 1956) found that level of academic attainment was not a good predictor of either interest or skill in reading. This finding may be taken to suggest that reading skill is to some extent separate from the kinds of ability developed and measured in formal education, and perhaps that reading develops well in a situation where real need or real interest demands it to be developed. However, these interpretations might in turn suggest that reading (at the silent level, at least) is either not well taught or is incapable of being taught, which seems unlikely.

A plausible explanation of the functional reading difficulties of undergraduates, and of those adults working in many commercial and other organizations who receive a course in reading as part of their training, is that schools do not equip their pupils very well for the reading demands of life after school. It might also be said that neither do they generate a great deal of interest in reading, for Chambers (1969) following an estimate in the Crowther report (CACE, 1959) suggests that 60% of the children leaving school never again read anything of any substance.

If it is accepted that secondary education does not lead to a desire to read and prepare fully for adult functional reading, there is clearly some cause for concern. It is true that if we say it is the fault of the schools we may seem to be indulging in the too common practice of passing the blame along the line, until eventually, of course, it rests in the parental home background of the early years. Such an activity is not very fruitful and in this case it is partly unjust for universities, for example, have a responsibility to help students develop further the skills they need at that level, quite apart from any remedial action which may be necessary. Nevertheless, there is a good deal of work which can be done in the middle school and the secondary school not only for intending university students but, more important perhaps, for those who leave school as soon as they are able and who will need to be able to read reasonably well if they are to pursue any further study.

Extent and role of silent reading in middle and secondary schools

It is not easy to gauge the proportion of time spent in secondary education on silent reading. A recent survey carried out at Nottingham University as part of a Schools Council project suggests that for a teacher to read aloud to a class becomes less common the higher one proceeds in the primary school, but that it then becomes common again in the early years of secondary education (Dolan and Harrison, 1975). Unfortunately for present purposes at least, the lack of distinction between oral and silent reading in the original data collection, and the failure to differentiate sustained reading from occasional reference to a text makes interpretation of the findings of this study difficult. Nevertheless, the picture is gained of there being little sustained silent reading, at least within schools.

A recent study of readers in primary and secondary schools in Scotland, did distinguish silent reading from oral reading (Maxwell, 1977). It was found that in primary schools both reading aloud to the teacher and set periods of silent reading were said by most teachers surveyed to be used regularly (as opposed to occasionally or not at all). In secondary schools there was a decline in the incidence of both reading aloud to the teacher and in formal silent reading, but the decline was less in the case of silent reading. Unfortunately, this study only enquired whether or not the activity occurred and thus casts no light on how sustained was the silent reading which occurred, or for what purpose it was employed.

It may also be noted from the survey in Scotland that the incidence of formal silent reading in secondary schools was closely matched by the incidence of the teacher reading aloud to the pupils. It could be argued, despite the increased use of individual project work, that schools are, by their organizational nature, places which lend themselves better to group listening activities than to more private ones such as silent reading.

Certainly the literature on the teaching of English places considerable emphasis on oral presentation of texts. A study of the use of books in English lessons in secondary schools (Calthrop, 1971) suggests that oral reading by teacher and pupil was quite a common activity in secondary education at the time of the survey. Indeed, Calthrop who argues for a shared experience of literature barely mentions private or silent reading. Less is written about the use of reading in subjects other than English in Britain, but it seems safe to assume that, at least before the sixth form, reading tends to be used as an aid for other means of presentation and that there is very little self-directed, private and uninterrupted use of texts for study.

Barnes *et al.* (1971) (speaking of literary texts) note the difficulty which children have simply in obtaining the general sense of what they read and this would seem to pose a dilemma for the English teacher who is concerned with higher levels of response. Possibly the teaching of literature itself suffers from the neglect of reading skill. However, one should be cautious of assuming that children do not read at all unless forced to do so. Numerous surveys of children's reading habits and interests (*see* Chapter 7) suggest that a great many secondary school children use their own time to read a wide and very eclectic choice of reading matter and spend considerable time in doing so.

It is becoming clear that there are certain apparent paradoxes and contradictions about reading in secondary education. One paradox is that reading in school is often a guided oral group activity where the reading is frequently interrupted, yet that this activity serves as a preparation for sustained, self-directed, silent and private reading whether for study or pleasure. Another contradiction is that pupils appear to read a great deal of their own accord, yet there is evidence that they are often reluctant to read in school and cease to do so on leaving formal education.

Reasons for the neglect of silent reading in schools

If schools are better suited to group activities, this no doubt contributes to the neglect of silent reading. Where it does take place, silent reading is difficult to observe, monitor and assess, and later chapters will deal with attempts to overcome these difficulties. There are also historical reasons for the neglect of silent reading, arising both from traditions in education which have affected the curriculum and from the historical development of silent reading itself as a medium.

There is no history of silent reading, and there are few histories of reading. However, those that there are (*see* e.g. Mathews, 1966; Davies, 1973) seem to be in agreement about the low status accorded to reading as a school subject up to, and sometimes including, recent times. Davies remarks that the early grammar schools did not consider it their job to help children who came unable to read, for it was the precise purpose of the Dame schools to attend to such a basic skill. In the nineteenth century it was a prime obligation of the elementary schools to ensure a certain standard of literacy, although the way this duty was interpreted and the results were assessed had unfortunate effects on education (*see* Matthew Arnold in e.g. Sutherland, 1973; also Goldstrom, 1972 and Hurt, 1971).

It is clear that those working at the higher levels of education did not in general concern themselves much with reading teaching. Furthermore, they were unlikely to pay attention to silent reading, for the type of reading done in the grammar and public schools seems to have been mainly oral reading or very close examination of a text. Indeed, it often was so outside education, for silent reading is a surprisingly modern activity even among the literate, as the next chapter indicates.

There has, therefore, at least in Britain, been no tradition of paying systematic attention to silent reading in secondary education; if anything, there appears to have been a deliberate policy of assigning reading tuition to the elementary school and its successors. This policy has perhaps been confirmed by the general reluctance of teachers of English to do anything which might undermine the hard-won status of the study of literature in schools. As histories of the teaching of English (see e.g. Shayer, 1972; Mathieson, 1975) show, there is and has been considerable confusion about what precisely should be taught in schools as English. Nevertheless, it is clear that concern for the academic respectability of the subject and the special role claimed for English teaching in personal development has led to an eschewing of teaching what might be seen as basic skills.

A final, related reason for the neglect of silent reading in education, appears to be the fact that many government reports have failed to agree on whose responsibility it is to ensure that reading skills are developed in secondary education. The influential Newbolt report (Board of Education, 1921) adopted the view enshrined in the frequently cited remark of George Sampson (Sampson, 1925) that every teacher is a teacher of English by dint of the fact that he teaches in English. The Bullock report (DES, 1975 esp. pp. 116-118 and 223) examines the question of who should have responsibility for developing the reading skills of 'normal' readers and concludes (largely from unfavourable impressions of specialized reading teaching in the United States) that it is the responsibility of every teacher to develop the reading skills necessary for his own subject. This may well be right in intention, but the report's own evidence shows that, even among teachers specializing in English, few are equipped for the task. It seems unlikely, therefore, that much change will result in practice from asking all teachers to take this responsibility.

Conclusion and summary

This chapter has argued that illiteracy is relative. It is not only those who are recognized as being in need of remedial help who should concern us, for we must also be aware of the reading difficulties encountered by those who succeed in the educational system. Such an awareness leads to a realization that there is little help given to children in developing silent reading in secondary education, and gives rise to questions as to why this should be so and as to what can be done to remedy the situation. Some reasons for the neglect have been suggested and some possible solutions emerge in the following chapters.

2

Silent Reading — an Historical Perspective

Although silent reading is not given adequate attention in British schools, it is precisely this aspect of reading which has most interested psychological researchers. During the early years of this century, research, often by eminent psychologists in the United States and some other countries, led indirectly to what might be termed a 'silent reading movement'. This chapter uses an historical framework to review both research and classroom practices up to about 1945.

Use of silent reading up to 1900

Silent reading was not a common activity in schools or elsewhere before the middle of the nineteenth century. It was almost unknown to the scholars of the classical and medieval worlds (Chaytor, 1945) and during the Renaissance the term 'reading' still undoubtedly connoted oral reading. It was only during the nineteenth century that silent reading became commonplace, possibly as Chaytor suggests (p. 19) because the British Museum reading room would be intolerably noisy if it were filled with the buzz of whispering and muttering which accompanied reading in the medieval monasteries.

There are other and more positive reasons than the need for silence in libraries to account for the development of silent reading. One is the gradual and steady increase in literacy during the nineteenth century (Cipolla, 1969). As the number of readers increased, so there was a relative decrease in the number of potential listeners for a text read aloud. As people became able to read for themselves, the volume and variety of printed material increased considerably. At the same time the reading of fiction and especially serious social commentary declined relatively, for the reading which predominated was of newspapers and other periodicals, and of specialized books often for self-improvement.

Webb (1958) remarks that after the Library Act of 1850, which gave rise to public libraries, the reading of light fiction became a lower middle class pursuit, whereas it was the artisans (industrial working class) who borrowed the solid books. Employers often encouraged their workers to study, with such effect that as early as the 1820s the rent of a village inn owned by the London Lead Company was regularly reduced, 'the miners preferring books to drink' (Raistrick and Jennings, 1965 p. 311).

The decline in literary reading and of a shared literary culture was much regretted by many nineteenth century commentators, and is indeed so regarded by many influential writers on the teaching of English (see e.g. Mathieson, 1975 for a review). However, whatever the merits of this culture, it barely survived the nineteenth century when it was overtaken by the more familiar culture, where printed mass media of general shared interest co-existed with books and periodicals for a specialized readership.

The change in the materials read and the uses to which reading was put necessitated different approaches to reading. Not only was oral reading often inappropriate, but it now became inefficient to use an oral style in reading, where every word of a text is read and where every book is read completely and sequentially. This style of silent reading was perhaps still appropriate and necessary for great fiction but it was with the intention of attacking those who advocated reading only great books that A. J. Balfour in 1887 rather misleadingly (and probably with deliberate irony) entitled his rectorial address to the students of St. Andrews 'The Pleasures of Reading' (Balfour, 1888). He stressed that reading should be eclectic and that authors should not be accorded undue deference. He parodied those who followed a reading scheme of 'great books', for their sole desire appeared to be to finish the books and their only reward self-denial. Apart from this apparent philistinism, he also had some interesting comments on how one should read. Skipping sections of books is not cheating, he asserted, and 'he has only half-learnt the art of reading who has not added to it the more refined accomplishments of skipping and skimming' (Balfour, 1888 p. 48).

Despite remarks such as these, the older oral approach to reading and the use of literary material continued to hold an important place in education for both practical and philosophical reasons, long after it had largely outlived its application in the outside world. Nevertheless, by the end of the nineteenth century considerable changes had taken place not only in what was read but also in how the reading was done. This is not to say, of course, that the matter of how and what to read was completely resolved or, even, that how to read was much discussed.

Early research into silent reading

If the revolution in reading methods and habits was as strong as has been argued, then it is hardly a coincidence that what are generally accepted as the earliest researches into silent reading were carried out in the late nineteenth century.

There were basically two lines of enquiry. One, which had fewer immediately apparent practical applications in the field of the teaching of reading, concentrated upon the study of eye-movements from the psychological standpoint. As E. B. Huey (1908) was to say in reviewing the early work, 'to completely analyse what we do when we read would almost be the acme of a psychologist's achievements for it would be to describe many of the most intricate workings of the human mind, as well as to unravel the tangled story of the most remarkable specific performance that civilization has learned in all its history' (Huey, 1908 p. 6). From the observation of Javal (1879) working in Paris, that the eyes when reading move not evenly but in fits and starts (*per saccades*), arose various experiments for which equipment was devised to monitor and record eye-movements. This scientific enquiry, which is still continuing, was less fruitful in leading to descriptions of the intricate workings of the human mind than at first appeared and, although this was rarely the researchers' intention, its effects on school practice, especially in the United States, were considerably greater than its contribution to psychological theory.

However, it was the linking of eye-movement research with another area, the measurement of reading speed, which led to the rethinking of reading teaching in American schools. Perhaps the earliest researcher into speed of reading was Romanes (1883) who, working in London and separately from Javal, gave subjects a marked paragraph in an opened book and asked them to read it. Romanes was mainly interested in reaction time, rather than what we now understand as speed of reading. However, the experiment is of great importance since, partly through misunderstandings in interpretation, it has given rise to a view still expressed in speed reading courses that speed of reading is not directly related to comprehension and that speed of reading is unrelated to intelligence.

Huey and his influence

Owing to the work of Huey in reporting the early experiments, as well as pursuing some of his own, these psychological researches came to have a considerable effect on American school practice. It is useful at this stage, therefore, to review briefly some of his findings and conclusions in the light of their influence on later attempts at teaching silent reading. Huey appears from his impressive and influential book *The Psychology and Pedagogy of Reading* to have been a researcher of broad interests who was concerned with the practical application of his findings, while at the same time retaining a curiosity and receptiveness which make his judgements still appear balanced, and as an editor of his facsimile reprint (Kolers, 1968) remarks, surprisingly up-to-date even now. Although it was prompted by what he called (Huey, 1908 p. 5) 'naive curiosity and the concern which we have for the penetration of mysteries', the book had both a concern for the teaching of reading and a considerable influence upon it. Apart from his general condemnation of school reading as 'an old curiosity shop of absurd practices', Huey's relevance for us in the present context lies in the importance which he attached to silent reading and, in particular, to the possibility of increasing speed or rate in silent reading. Related to this were his interests in eye-movement studies, in sub-vocal activity during reading, and in the question of whether reading improvement is largely a matter of visual technique.

Huey devotes considerable space to the question, much debated since, of whether purely visual reading is possible or whether reading is inevitably accompanied by some form of inner speech. Although he considers purely visual reading theoretically possible, he finds it unsurprising that subjects tend to read aloud more slowly than when they are reading silently. As will be seen, later American writers were to assume that sub-vocalization slows the reader and is undesirable, but Huey distinguished between lip-movement which accompanies *sotto voce* oral reading, and the vestigial inner speech which he considered universal or nearly so. The presence or absence of sub-vocalization is most likely to be of less concern at the practical level than it appeared to be to Huey, and to others, who were later to attempt to suppress it in silent reading.

The question of whether rate of reading is merely a matter of visual technique is altogether more important. Huey was inclined to accept the conclusions of Romanes already mentioned, although he did not go so far as some later writers who have assumed that anyone, whatever their intelligence, may read quickly and that comprehension does not decline with speed. Closer examination of Romanes' own report (Romanes, 1883 pp. 136–137) reveals, however, that Huey was a little uncritical in generalizing from a small number of subjects whose task was to read one paragraph (not *paragraphs* as Huey says) and were given 20 seconds 'from cold' for the task. Huey mentions four other relevant studies in his chapter on increasing speed, but none suggests that speed is independent of intelligence, for they merely show that there is a general superiority of recall among those who read faster.

One aspect of Huey's review which was to have bearing on the teaching of reading, and is also relevant to the question of whether speed reading is solely or mainly a matter of technique, is in his interpretation of the eye-movements of rapid readers. He found that their eyes appeared to settle to a regular rhythmical pattern when reading a number of pages and Huey explained this regularity following Dearborn (1906) in terms of short-lived motor habits. According to Dearborn the eye falls into a brief motor habit which often results in the reader's making a certain number of pauses per line independently of variations in the subject matter from line to line. Dearborn considered that establishing regular rhythmical movement was important for developing reading rate. Much later these views were to lead to his jointly devising (Dearborn and Anderson, 1937) the Harvard reading films, although later still he was to seriously question the value of these and other mechanical aids to reading improvement (Anderson and Dearborn, 1952).

Huey did not advocate eye-training *per se*, although he contrasted the rhythm of Dearborn's subjects with the slower approach 'set and hardened in the days of listless poring over uninteresting texts, or in imitation of the slow reading aloud which was usually going on either with ourselves or with others in the school' (p. 179). Thus it was to habits developed in school reading that he attributed the problems encountered by adults. Ironically, however, in view of the work of some of his followers, the means he used to rectify his own slow rate consisted of no more than 'waking up to the fact that my own reading was unnecessarily slow, and then persistently reading as fast as possible with well concentrated attention, taking care to stop short of fatigue until the new pace was somewhat established' (p.179).

Origins of the silent reading movement

For Huey one of the more absurd practices in school was the emphasis on oral reading and in this respect his influence on schools was fairly rapid. A few years after the publication of Huey's book, Nila Banton Smith was able to say in her book entitled *One Hundred Ways of Teaching Silent Reading* that 'at the present time the young American is given extensive training in the *silent* reading of *all kinds of materials* and for a *great variety of purposes*' (Smith, 1925 p.1, original italics). The extensive nature of the training was perhaps overstated but the book provides a wide range of games and activities involving silent reading for children in grades 1 to 8 (i.e. 6 to 13 years old).

Another indication of the fact that silent reading was being taken seriously is an experiment by O'Brien (1921) intended to determine the factors influencing the rate of reading of children in grades 3 to 8 i.e. between ages 8 to 13. Adopting what might now be called an action research approach he attempted to increase their rate of reading by means of one of three types of training. One group was given only practice and encouragement; another group was given practice and encouragement and also encouraged to avoid vocalization; the third was also to be given practice and encouragement and, in addition, training to enlarge the perceptual span (of words per fixation). Problems in the execution of the experiment and weaknesses in its basic design dictate caution in interpreting the findings, but it is interesting to note that there was little difference between the groups, that a doubling of speed was fairly common among subjects, but that a plateau was reached beyond which it was difficult to progress further. Checks on comprehension were superficial, but there seemed to be grounds for thinking that these children had been accustomed to reading unnecessarily slowly.

O'Brien's report is, however, more valuable for its review of the then current literature, and for his identification of factors affecting reading rate, than for his own empirical study. A fuller critical review is given elsewhere (Pugh, 1974) but it may be noted here that O'Brien subscribed to the view that reading rate is largely determined by visual, rather than central mental factors, and can, therefore, be fairly readily trained.

As a result of this emphasis on visual behaviour in much of the work of the period, the improvement of silent reading came to be seen as a rather technical and somewhat peripheral activity and not as part of the main work of the school. As already noted, the Bullock report (DES, 1975) criticized the present American approach on these grounds, and it is unfortunate that those concerned with silent reading in the 1920s did not pay more attention to the correction of the root causes of the problem as perceived by Huey. Nevertheless, they succeeded in establishing the importance of silent reading in education and also provided some practical suggestions for helping in the development of silent reading.

Influence of the silent reading movement

The first published reading improvement course for adults (Pitkin, 1929) was produced at the end of the 1920s and the influence of the work of O'Brien, Nila Banton Smith and other writers of the time is apparent in the assumptions underlying this and most other courses of the speed reading type. As is argued in the following chapters, the assumptions are on the whole untested and are simplifications of highly questionable and much debated psychological issues. One fact which does seem to emerge is that although rate of reading is rather unstable (at least in situations where one attempts to measure it) it nevertheless tends to increase with directed practice.

Thus, the main result of the early study of silent reading in *schools* was, oddly enough, to give rise to courses intended to help *adults* improve their reading rate or, in American schools, to lead to specialized silent reading activities. Apart from this the main American work of interest up to 1945 which is relevant to silent reading is the attempt made by McDade and Buswell to teach beginning reading entirely by non-oral methods. James E. McDade, as Assistant Superintendent of Schools in Chicago, was able to provide a considerable number of subjects (70,000 between 1935 and 1945) for one of the most large-scale experiments in the teaching of reading. Buswell, who reported the experiment (Buswell, 1945), was a well-known psychologist who had worked in the Adult Reading Clinic at the University of Chicago and came to believe 'without qualification that the largest single obstacle to efficient reading for these adults is the tendency to sub-vocalize and proceed word by word as they read' (1945 p. 4). One should be cautious in accepting evidence based on observations of adults as justification for a method of teaching initial reading, as Marchbanks and Levin (1965) warn in another context. Nevertheless, Buswell held that inner speech need not accompany adult reading, even though some of the 'older schools of psychological thinking' held that it did (Buswell, 1945 p. 4).

The results of the experiment, during which considerable numbers of beginning readers in their first two years at school were prevented as far as possible from reading aloud, indicated that by grade IV (i.e. age 10) 17% of those taught initially by the non-oral method showed overt signs of vocalization as against 21% of those taught by conventional methods. The results are not very conclusive for various reasons, and the design is weak since it seems unlikely, for example, that children would have had no recourse to reading aloud outside school. More important perhaps, is the fact that the experiment provides no evidence that vocalization is, in fact, harmful or undesirable at this stage. It merely suggests that, in certain situations at least, overt sub-vocalization can be reduced.

Influence of the silent reading movement on British education

The American researches into silent reading were known to psychologists in Britain and M. D. Vernon (1931) provided a thorough review of them. However, as Shayer (1972) shows in his history of the teaching of English in British schools, the British emphasis was rather different from the American. As it came to be realized in Britain that skill in reading aloud was not the only type of reading of importance, so from about 1910 there was an increased use of comprehension exercises. These differed from the kind of exercises used in American schools, in that they required careful reading and study and encouraged reference back to the text. Also they were unspeeded, whereas American exercises were often texts which the pupil should read only once, often under timed conditions, before proceeding to answer questions from what he could recall of what he had read. Thus speed of silent reading was not of great concern to British teachers and Shayer, although he is aware of the American work, makes no mention of speed as an aspect of reading of interest to British teachers of English during the period covered by his history (1900–1970).

Perhaps the only British writer concerned with teaching who was directly influenced by the work of O'Brien and others is Michael West (West, 1926), himself to become a highly influential writer on the teaching of English as a foreign language. West, who was working in Bengal, is particularly interesting for his attempts to ensure transfer from reading skills learned in school to the reading needs of adult life and also because of his perception of the role of reading in the whole language curriculum. His work still warrants reading by those concerned with teaching reading in this country even though its influence on British schools was negligible. A particularly valuable practical idea of West's was to elicit different types of reading by varying the 'question density', as he called it. The relevance of questions in setting purposes for reading, and the importance of varying reading style according to purpose, tended to be overlooked by American researchers as will be seen in subsequent chapters.

For the present we may conclude that American psychological researches and curriculum experiments in the teaching of silent reading had very little effect or influence on British education and did not lead to the teaching of silent reading in schools. In other countries, notably Belgium, the influence was considerable (for reasons given by Burion 1968; *see also* Wiomont, 1960 and

Segers, 1962). There, as in France, silent reading games and exercises are used, in some schools at least, as part of reading work from very early in a child's school career. In Britain, there are strong reasons why many teachers of English would be reluctant to follow these examples and might be loathe to accept West's needs-based curriculum. This would have been especially so at a time when Sampson (1925) and others were arguing for the importance of literature as a means of preparing *against* life after school.

Conclusion and summary

Silent reading was given little attention by psychologists until the latter years of the last century, when as a mode of reading it was still a fairly recent development. Early psychological research, which was not intended to have applications in schools and which believed it had found in reading a very suitable medium for psychological study, nevertheless led in the United States to a great deal of interest in teaching silent reading. The considerable amount of work done in American schools between approximately 1910 and 1930 led, however, to reading becoming a specialized subject rather than to the reappraisal of the use and teaching of reading in schools which Huey appeared to be calling for. It also led to speed reading courses for adults, of which more will be said in chapters 4 and 5. The influence of the American work on Britain was slight, as we had already opted for comprehension exercises requiring close textual study and because other strong trends were developing in English teaching which were contrary to the American approach.

From the work reviewed in this chapter a number of questions arise. The most important is whether the teaching of silent reading must necessarily be carried out by means of specialist exercises with the risk that there will be little or no transfer to realistic situations. Alternatively, the Bullock report may be right in making the teaching of reading in his own subject area the responsibility of every subject teacher. Another related issue is whether the considerable amount of psychological research into silent reading has contributed much of practical use to the teacher who wishes to help develop silent reading. Finally, arising from Buswell's experiment in non-oral reading is the question of the age at which silent reading should begin. These points are taken up again in subsequent chapters, where there is also discussion of more recent attempts to teach silent reading.

3

Recent Approaches to Beginning Silent Reading

The teaching of silent reading before the second world war was not, on the whole, seen within any developmental framework. Children and adults, as well as foreign language learners with various degrees of skill, were given exercises and courses to increase their speed of reading. The concern at that time seems to have been almost with speed for its own sake. Since the theoretical basis for speed reading training, though dubious, appeared to be highly scientific, it is not surprising that attention was distracted from the fact that most adult reading, and probably much children's reading also, is purposeful and, hence, can be strategic. In other words, reading straight through a text, at whatever rate, may well be the worst way on many occasions of achieving one's goal in reading efficiently.

To think of silent reading as merely *sotto voce* oral reading is misleading and unhelpful. It is true that, even with this view of reading, a reader has many advantages over a non-reader, since he has access to a wide range of information which is conveniently available at most times and in most places. He has no need for playback devices, since in a sense he is one, and he is not at the mercy of media programme planners. He may, either mentally or by making notes, store the information he obtains in the code in which it was originally stored, although it will limit learning if he feels constrained to keep too closely to the linguistic form of the original text in his own notes.

The view of the reader as a playback device or as a mere receptor of other men's words is restrictive, and in true silent reading he is not obliged to read in this way. There the reader is self-paced, or at least may vary his pace and approach in the light of the inter-action between himself and the text. Thus, his degree of speed and attention can be varied according to his needs and purposes, although he may be to some extent limited by his own abilities and constrained by the author's method of presentation. Nevertheless he has a great deal more freedom than is conceded by McLuhan (1967), who stresses the effect on thought of linear presentation in print. As Morris (1963) points out, the skilled adult silent reader is not involved necessarily in a linear and sequential process akin to listening or to oral reading, and as I. A. Richards suggested (1924, p. 1) the reader can use a book as 'a machine to think with'.

For the purposes of helping adults and undergraduates develop their efficiency in silent reading, this emphasis on the flexibility available to the adult has seemed important as will be seen in later chapters. The question now arises as to whether the teaching of skills used by adults is the best way of developing those skills in children. It has already been pointed out (Chapter 2) that there are dangers in assuming that the adult provides a model to be copied as opposed to indicating what a child must attain; as remarked elsewhere (Pugh, 1975a), the adult illiterate is often adept at copying the visual and observable behaviour of the skilled reader. There may, therefore, be necessarily indirect routes towards skilled adult silent reading.

Models of reading development

The past fifty years or so have seen a considerable amount of theoretical and empirical work in the field of reading. Indeed, Farr and Weintraub (1975) indicate that nearly as much reading research was published in the twelve months up to June 1974, as in the whole period up to 1925. Nevertheless, models of reading development tend to be incomplete, perhaps because as Geyer (1972) concludes, from his review of 48 models of the reading process, we have insufficient understanding of the processes involved in reading to permit us to apply most of the models to normal reading. This difficulty in observing reading behaviour and the question of ensuring and assessing transfer of learning from courses to realistic reading tasks will be discussed more fully later, but for the present it should be noted that most theories of reading development tend to examine beginning readers and adult readers but to say little about the stages in between.

Certain recent writers, especially those with a psycholinguistic approach, stress that reading involves information processing (*see* e.g. Smith, 1971, 1973) as well as (or instead of) oral production. They have focussed more attention upon this in-between stage than earlier writers and the role of increasing knowledge of language structures has been particularly emphasised. However, Gibson (1972), while accepting that the growth of reading ability is related to the growth of knowledge of structure, nevertheless considers that the way in which the reader incorporates his developing knowledge of structure in his reading habits remains a mystery.

Nevertheless, a working model of reading development which has been found useful in a number of studies is based on one proposed by the psycholinguist Kenneth Goodman. Goodman (1968) suggested that there are basically three stages in the development of reading skill. The stages overlapped and indeed were not discrete in another sense, in that one might revert to an earlier stage according to factors such as difficulty in a text. The stages as given by Goodman involved a decrease in the attention to detail necessary for reading increasingly larger units of text (e.g. letters, words etc.) as one grows more proficient. What is perhaps most interesting though, is that he proposed three different styles of processing at the three stages. At the first stage a number of processes are needed in oral reading to obtain meaning. The in-between stage is a (noiseless) listening-in to the text, possibly with some attempt to reconstitute it for purposes of 'listening'. At the third, silent reading, meaning is obtained much more directly. (Adult oral reading is seen as a rather specialized activity, different from earlier oral reading, and thus it does not concern us for the moment in considering this model.)

Thus Goodman, contrary to Buswell (1945) implies that silent reading should be preceded by oral reading. Furthermore, he suggests that in the transfer from oral to silent reading there is a stage at which the text is reconstituted for the reader's own ear, although not for the benefit of listeners. Whether this trace of sub-vocal activity or inner speech ever completely disappears is highly controversial. Gibson and Levin (1975) consider that it does. Conrad (1972) reviewed the literature and also reported on studies of his own. He seemed to consider that it did not normally disappear, but that the more interesting question was the function of inner speech. Edfeldt (1959) considered it harmful to

attempt to suppress sub-vocalization and inner speech, thus disagreeing with Buswell by whom he had earlier been influenced. Sokolov (1960 and 1968) considered it inevitable and useful but Gibson and Levin (1975) criticize his interpretations as too much influenced by the Russian tradition in psychology, which most certainly does consider inner speech of more importance than do the American researchers.

As noted in the discussion of Huey in Chapter 2, the question may appear to be of little practical importance for reading at the silent level. However, it becomes important if one accepts the standard American textbook view that inner speech is harmful in silent reading at earlier stages, for then this listening-in stage derived from Goodman's model might be seen to be a stage which should be as short as possible in duration. On the other hand, the existence of the stage might indicate that reading in this way should be nurtured in order to help progress from oral to silent reading.

Some evidence for the existence of an 'aural' stage, as this listening-in stage has been called, is given by Neville and Pugh (1974, 1976). In these studies middle-school children were given cloze tests of reading and parallel cloze tests of either listening or restricted reading. (A cloze test consists of a passage or passages from which words have been deleted at certain intervals. Those taking the test attempt to supply the missing words.) The restricted reading test was in the form of a booklet which had to be proceeded through sequentially. The information for the listening test was also received sequentially, of course, in the order in which the author wrote the text, but in the normal reading test children could move backwards or forwards within the text. Various rather detailed linguistic analyses of mistakes were attempted but what is mainly of interest here is the finding relating to differences in behaviour when the subjects in the upper half according to reading score were compared with those in the lower half. It was found that the mode of presentation produced significantly different scores for those who did better than average on the reading test, but not in the case of those who did worse. An interpretation of this is that the better readers could use silent reading strategies and were not obliged to read sequentially. The poorer readers, however, were reading in a manner in many ways like that employed in oral reading or listening, rather than truly silently, although to all outward appearances all subjects read silently during the testing.

A recent study by Mosenthal (1976) also investigates whether reading and listening require similar skill or processing, at least at certain ages. Mosenthal used syllogisms for listening, reading aloud and reading silently with 7- and 8-year-old children. He concludes that oral reading requires different 'comprehension competence' from listening or 'silent' reading. It should be noted, however, that with children of this age it may well be 'aural' rather than truly silent reading which was employed.

On the broader question of the relationship between reading and listening, the evidence is conflicting (see Weintraub, 1972 for annotated references). It seems bound to be so if one attempts to generalize from subjects of very different ages, thus taking no account of the stages which appear to exist in reading development. Similarly, the use of materials for listening which closely resemble written texts may be misleading, as is noted by Wilkinson (1969) and by Walker (1976) who, in reporting a study comparing reading with spontaneous speech, discusses the problem more fully.

Approaches to developing reading fluency

Despite uncertainty about the relationship between reading and listening, the possible existence of an aural stage suggests that reading while listening may be a feasible method for developing reading fluency. This approach, whereby a child listens to a recording of a text which at the same time he follows visually, appears to be becoming increasingly popular. The BBCs *Listening and Reading* materials are perhaps the best known. A full survey of materials available in Britain is given in an annotated bibliography (Daly, Neville and Pugh, 1975) which also reviews empirical studies of the use of reading while listening.

The approach has also been used with overseas students whose English proficiency was low (Neville and Pugh, 1975a) and for an introductory course for new overseas students at the University of Leeds (see Pugh, 1975b). Here it was found to be more successful than courses which relied on silent reading exercises and it was felt that the aural input from the tape-recording may have helped in the understanding of the text.

There is other evidence (*see* Narayanaswamy, 1973; Pugh, 1976) which suggests that attempts to develop reading fluency in overseas students by means of practice in silent reading may be unhelpful. However, these students are in a different situation from that of the native English-speaking child who is not able to read fluently in any language.

For English children, the evidence suggests that the approach does help poorer readers at the beginning of middle school, but that it is of more help to some than others. In one study, the post-test variance of those who had used listening while reading was found to be significantly greater than that of a control group (Neville and Pugh, 1975b) although mean improvement was similar. It has also been found (Neville and Pugh, 1978) that the approach can be used with great economy of teacher time. Other studies have also found the approach useful (*see* Daly, Neville and Pugh, 1975) although interpreting findings requires caution. Not least it is necessary to know what tests were used for measurement and whether these can fairly be used as a measure of reading fluency. Since, as the later chapter on testing indicates, there is a paucity of suitable tests, the GAP cloze test (McLeod and Unwin, 1970) was used in the studies by Neville and Pugh. There may, however, be other effects from the use of reading while listening which ought to be measured. In some work currently in progress (and briefly mentioned in Pugh, 1977a) an attempt has been made to assess broader effects, such as arousal of interest in reading.

Long-term effects need also to be examined, since some of the literature referred to earlier might be taken to suggest that encouraging a relationship between the appearance of words and their sounds can hinder the development of silent reading skills. This possibility has been discounted as unlikely for reasons given elsewhere (Neville and Pugh, 1975a), but empirical evidence is needed nonetheless. A more difficult question related to the effect of reading while listening, is the age or stage of reading development at which the approach should be employed. Possibly there is no simple answer to this, since the difficulty of the recorded text and the purpose in using it may need to be taken into account. It has been found (Neville, 1975) that the rate at which the text is presented in itself appears to affect its difficulty and this adds to the problem. Nevertheless, there are grounds for thinking that it is in the late primary school or early middle and secondary school that there is the greatest need to develop fluency in sequential reading as a preparation for true silent reading.

A different approach to developing fluency is suggested by Merritt (1970) who uses the term 'intermediate skills' and advocates the use of cloze procedure as a method for developing reading at this in-between stage. Cloze procedure was originally advocated as a measure of readability by Taylor (1953). Although it has been much used in teaching, Jongsma (1971) indicates in his review of the literature that cloze procedure has not been carefully assessed as a teaching technique. A major difficulty lies once more in the lack of suitable tests of reading fluency, and hence in the use of cloze tests to determine the effect of cloze programmes. Clearly there is some danger in this approach and Jongsma concludes that there must be doubt about the value of cloze for teaching. Its use in developing reading fluency is certainly questionable, since the kind of reading it demonstrates, and hence might appear to advocate, is very different indeed from fluent reading. Although cloze procedure has several uses, some of them related to teaching, its unconsidered use illustrates the danger of confusing a research and testing technique with a teaching method.

The two approaches mentioned so far have been specifically concerned with the stage between oral and silent reading. Other approaches give practice, often motivated practice, in silent reading usually accompanied by other activities. They tend to cover a wider age range and not to attempt to make the distinction of the intermediate or 'aural stage'. However, insofar as they involve sequential reading of a text and are intended to be of use beyond the oral reading stage, they are relevant here. The best known specially prepared materials are the SRA reading laboratories. Somewhat similar materials have been published by Drake Educational Associates, Longman, and Ward Lock. (*See* Appendix.)

As with listening while reading and cloze procedure, it is not intended that reading laboratories should form all of a child's reading work in school, but rather that they should be used judiciously alongside other materials. The SRA materials are in the tradition of the games and activities of the American silent reading movement (Chapter 2) and consist of graded work cards which children work through keeping their own records of comprehension scores and results of other activities. Rate of reading is given some attention. The marking is done by the children themselves and hence they receive immediate feedback. The quality of the feedback in this kind of material has been questioned (Pugh, 1976) because there appears to be no recognition of the inherent difficulties in testing accurately and reliably factors such as speed and comprehension in reading (*see* Chapter 8). Others have criticized the SRA materials on the grounds of the inappropriateness of their (American) subject matter, their minimal literary quality and the arbitrary nature of the purpose given for reading. Despite some generally unfavourable opinions about these materials—including doubts expressed in the Bullock report about transfer of learning from them (DES, 1975, pp. 117 and 120)—the findings of the Schools Council Project at Nottingham University (reported in Lunzer, 1976; Fawcett, 1977) indicate that with a large sample of secondary schoolchildren the experimental group using SRA material made significant gains as measured on various tests when compared with the control group. The difference was found both in the short term and in the longer term.

As Lunzer notes, there may be factors in the SRA materials which help and develop test taking. This may account for the fact that in a subsidiary experiment the SRA materials were found to be much more effective than the British Ward Lock materials which in some ways resemble them. There appears also to be no real evidence of transfer of learning to other situations. Nevertheless, there are grounds for thinking that, as with exercises in cloze procedure, they may help some children to become motivated to read and thus gain confidence.

Conclusion and summary

The concern here has been to distinguish true silent reading from oral reading and from 'aural' reading. It has been argued that what is often meant by reading fluency is in fact 'aural' reading. Certain approaches, namely cloze and reading while listening, which have been advocated by some writers as being particularly appropriate for this stage have been examined, although here the use of cloze procedure in developing reading fluency has been questioned. Reading laboratories may be of help in developing sequential fluent reading at the aural or reading fluency stage, though there is debate about their value.

In view of the lack of knowledge about developmental stages in reading much of this chapter is tentative, yet the distinction between a sequential style of reading and the type of reading undertaken by an effective adult reader seems an important one. Moreover, it appears that it may well be necessary in ensuring a sound basis for developing silent reading, to take account of the aural stage, just as *pace* Buswell, the oral stage seems necessary to begin with.

4

Speed Reading Courses—a Critical Review

It appears that speed reading is still fairly widely taught in American schools (*see* e.g. Miller, 1972) whereas in Britain there is very little evidence of schools paying attention to speed of reading, although it is mentioned in an early Schools Council Working Paper on English teaching (Schools Council 1965). The Bullock report, comprehensive as it is, barely mentions reading speed and only a few accounts of attempts to increase British children's speed of reading are available (*see* e.g. Watts and Buzan, 1973; and Wood, 1971). These are of limited value since they relate to the use or adaptation of commercially designed courses intended originally for adults.

Rather more use has been made of speed reading courses in further education and in higher education in Britain, although here again the attention to speed reading has been less than in North America. There, both in Canada (Hayward, 1971) and in the United States (Shaw, 1961) it appears that many colleges and universities have well established courses to help students improve speed of reading and other reading skills. Indeed, it may be because of this application of the courses that study skills frequently feature in them, and that courses often play down their emphasis on speed.

Although some features of speed reading courses may be adapted for use with schoolchildren and students, the courses have considerable shortcomings. However, they deserve examination here, since speed reading is the one area of silent reading which has received a considerable amount of attention from teachers and researchers. Furthermore, an understanding of how speed reading courses work not only helps temper uncritical enthusiasm but it can also lead to clarification of what a more worthwhile course might contain and how such a course might be taught.

This chapter provides a review of a number of courses intended to help students and businessmen increase their speed of reading. However, rather than reviewing the courses individually, reference is made to a wide range of courses so that comparisons can be made, common features noted and differences highlighted.

Types of speed reading courses available

Speed reading courses are available in published form as books or kits, and also as 'tutored courses'. The tutored courses are sometimes made available to employees of large organizations as part of their training, but they are also available to the general public through a number of agencies. In Britain these have included university extra-mural departments and colleges of further education but the better known courses are those offered by commercial concerns which specialize in giving courses for a fee, which is usually considerable. Reviews of courses given in Britain include those by Poulton (1961), and a consumer review in *Which* (1968).

The published courses appear to originate very often in tutored courses. Also, at least one of these has been adapted for television. Entitled *Use Your Head* (Buzan, 1974) it contains some material similar to that in the author's book on speed reading (Buzan, 1971) and is also akin to courses which Buzan has given at the University of Sussex (*see* Watts 1969, 1972). Television-based courses have been more widely used in the United States (Schale, 1971) and some attempts have also been made to use video-taped courses.

Aims of speed reading courses

The tutored courses offered by commercial concerns usually offer a guarantee that reading speed will triple as a result of taking the course. According to advertising brochures issued in 1972, Evelyn Wood Reading Dynamics claims to 'teach you to read 3–10 times faster' and to 'improve your powers of comprehension and recall'. This course consisted of eight three-hour sessions, cost £59 in 1972, and the organizers gave an assurance that 'the institute will refund a student's entire tuition fee if, after completing the minimum set class and study requirements, he fails to triple his reading efficiency as measured by our beginning and ending tests'. A similar guarantee was offered in 1968 by another commercial concern Dynamic Reading. Watts (1969, 1972) reporting on these courses at the University of Sussex, found the claims on the whole to be justified. However, Watts did not treat his data statistically, nor did he do so in a report by Watts and Buzan (1973) on the College of Advanced Reading course given to a group of twenty-nine grammar school girls in the fifth and sixth forms. Here only four of the girls failed to show a threefold increase in speed, but statistical examination (using a sign test) revealed no significant change in comprehension score from pre-test to post-test.

Other tutored courses tend to claim lower gains in speed, although they are similar in aim. According to the teacher's manual (Gregory, 1966) the prime objective of the Carborundum *Effective Reading* course is proficiency in reading, but the manual and indeed the first exercise on the course, stress speed and argue that comprehension tends to increase with speed. Examination of the results collected by Poulton (1961) from a number of Harvard film-aided courses reveals that speed in conjunction with comprehension was the only factor taken into account by tutors in assessing performance on a course. This is hardly surprising, since it is consistent with the method of presentation of this type of course in which there is a tachistoscopic type of exposure of text on motion film. The effect is that the viewer sees the text exposed in phrases, the duration of which is predetermined so that he is forced to read, if he reads at all, at a set speed. In the Carborundum course this is gradually increased from approximately 100 words per minute to approximately 1,000 words per minute. It is fair to point out, however, that speeds in excess of 600 words per minute are regarded by Gregory as involving skimming rather than fast reading.

Wainwright's course in efficient reading, as taught in further education and later published in revised form (Wainwright, 1968) advocates aiming at a doubling of reading speed without loss of comprehension. Wainwright (1967) has reported average gains in speed of 95% and in comprehension of 8% in courses held in the 1965–66 session at Hebburn Technical College, County Durham. The tests used were taken from Fry's drill book which was primarily intended for use in African Colleges and Universities (Fry, 1963b) and the findings are not treated statistically. It is also not clear whether the comprehension increase is expressed in terms of mean additional percentage points obtained or whether it is expressed as a percentage of the original average score. The comment about lack of statistical treatment also applies to fuller data produced earlier by Wainwright (1965). Poulton (1961) had found difficulty in obtaining data from use in Britain of the Harvard courses (Perry and Whitlock, 1948a and b) for statistical testing and the impression is gained, in Britain at least, that statistical treatment of data obtained from courses is rare. Maxwell (1971) implies that this is also true in the United States.

However, the objective of doubling or tripling of reading speed without loss of comprehension as measured by questions after reading seems to be commonly achieved on those tests used on the courses. Although the courses aim to offer other benefits, such as increased concentration, better study habits and increased retention, these are subsidiary in their advertising and in reports of their students' achievements. The only specific behavioural objectives which are stated relate to speed and comprehension on the tests used; and for the student the emphasis on speed must be reinforced by his regularly taking tests of speed during, as well as before and after, a course.

With the exception of that of Diack (1964) all the published courses examined also mention speed of reading at or near the beginning. For many speed is used as if it were synonymous with quality. Leedy (1956) for example, begins (p. 1) by asking 'So you want to read better? You want to read faster, with greater comprehension?' Yorkey (1970) in his study skills course for overseas students, seems to regard slow reading as synonymous with poor reading. He says (p. 91) 'If you read slowly you will have to spend too much time reading your assignments so that your other work may suffer. Poor reading may be a problem for you, but it is not a hopeless one.'

Many of the courses seem eager to persuade the reader that he wishes to read faster. It is, perhaps, reasonable enough, in view of the fact that his book is entitled *Rapid Reading*, that Dudley (1964) should begin by informing the reader: 'You have picked up this book because you want to be able to read faster.' (p. 15). Other courses are less direct, but a very common way of beginning a course is to refer to various alarming estimates of the growing amount of material published in the modern world and then to offer, as a solution, training in reading more rapidly. Some published courses exhibit a broader concern and try to improve comprehension as well. However, it usually emerges that what is meant by comprehension is merely the ability to answer questions set by the course deviser. Few of the courses attempt to improve (as opposed to maintaining) even the comprehension which is measured in this way. Zielke (1965), however, claims to have done so on his tutored courses in Germany and thus implies that it is possible in his published course too. Most courses state fairly early on that comprehension tends to increase with speed if it changes at all, and leave the question at that.

One of the courses, that of de Leeuw and de Leeuw (1965), is unusual in that it plays down the importance of speed on its opening page and claims that the emphasis is on purpose, comprehension and method of assimilation. On the next page, however, (p. 10) the authors conclude their preface with the following remarks which can give the reader the impression that speed is very important:

> The improvement in reading speed, according to the ability to comprehend short passages, is truly astonishing; but this increase in efficiency is small in comparison with the saving in time and effort that is possible where the reader has more opportunity to become a strategist; he may, in fact, be able to double or even to treble his volume of reading.

De Leeuw and de Leeuw are, however, running counter to much of their own text by stating their behavioural objectives in terms of speed, even if here they are concerned with rate of reading in books rather than in the tests. Yet the predominance of short passages followed by questions in their book does appear to give prominence to reading speed. The problem is that speed of reading is usually considered to be by far the most readily measurable aspect of adult reading, although the apparent simplicity of measurement is misleading. Comprehension is much less easily measured for there are no agreed scales and many factors operate to cause fluctuation in the difficulty of questions. Comprehension questions can, at best, do no more than sample the product of any reading and of the thinking which accompanies it; the sampling must cause simplification and distortion of the product of the complex activities involved in reading. Problems of this kind have ensured that even the most thoughtful courses have found their objectives dominated by a concern for increase in speed of reading, tempered only in part by a concern for avoiding a loss (as opposed to ensuring improvement) in measured comprehension.

Examination of the stated or implied objectives of courses with names such as speed reading, rapid reading, efficient reading, better reading, and so on, reveals that the main difference between the measurable objectives of courses is in the degree of speed increase which is considered possible without loss of comprehension. Some of the courses suggest that a 50 per cent improvement is likely (Witty (1953); de Leeuw and de Leeuw (1965)). However, Waldman (1958), arguing from the premise that people read at only 20 to 25 per cent of capacity, accepts the lower of his percentages and calculates that by working at only 50 per cent of capacity an improvement in rate of 150 per cent can be achieved. The basis for calculation is perhaps a little dubious, but the high expectations are similar to those expressed in commercial courses and in some German published courses, for example, which consider a doubling or trebling of rate to be possible. The British published courses are on the whole rather more cautious, regarding a doubling of speed as the most that is likely to be achieved.

A few of the courses try to consider speed and comprehension together when assessing efficiency in reading. Leedy (1956), for example, uses a quotient derived from multiplying reading rate by fractional percentage comprehension. Diack (1964) has devised his own rather complicated scale whereby points are awarded for comprehension but are then modified to some extent in the light of the time taken to read a passage for which a 'time-base' has been pre-determined. Anderson (1969) is unusual in timing the comprehension questions for some of his exercises; most courses permit unlimited time for answering comprehension questions.

Apart from the concern with speed of reading, or less commonly with 'speed of comprehension', the courses offer

advice intended to change behaviour in a number of areas. Many of the courses follow the early example of Pitkin (1929) and advise on physical and environmental factors affecting reading and study. Many also follow him in treating skimming as a specialized form of reading, although rather few have elaborated upon, or even accepted, the division of reading into different types which are related to the reader's purpose. Pitkin's names for types of reading, (light, average, solid and heavy) are not very helpful labels but it is interesting to note that the idea of adapting speed to purpose and to the type of subject matter was present in the earliest published course, although it tends to be absent from later courses.

Some courses do, of course, mention reading purpose but the use of different approaches for different purposes is rarely made very clear. Skimming, for example, is nearly always treated as a skill in its own right, although its use in previewing and revising material as part of an approach to studying a text is advocated in some of the courses. Advice on some rather specific reading tasks is offered in a few of the courses; Leedy (1956), for example, follows his chapter on how to read a newspaper with a chapter on reading graphs, maps, charts and other visual aids.

Many of the courses give advice on memory and on study technique. This tends in some cases not to be closely related to the advice on reading although the de Leeuws, for example, do attempt to give exercises in which the student may apply some of their recommendations. One difficulty with much of the advice given on how to read is that it is not clear to what extent it constitutes a general admonition for all reading tasks and to what extent it applies only to the particular task being undertaken at a certain stage of the course. In an attempt to make the tasks appear more genuine, and thus encourage various approaches with a realistic purpose, a few of the courses (e.g. Webster (1964), Diack (1964)) use the actual text of the book as practice material.

In whatever way the courses attempt to overcome the problems of narrowness of scope and limitations on the extent to which advice can be generalized, the fact remains that all courses pay considerable and regular attention to speed of reading. Thus even when the stated aim of a course is broader than simply increasing speed without loss of comprehension on the tests given, the difficulty of measuring other behavioural objectives results in their being dominated by the pursuit of greater speeds.

Methods used in tutored courses

Tutored courses consist of a number of sessions which usually include practice, talks by the tutor and some discussion. Sometimes films and other pacing devices are used. The use of films is of doubtful value and has, as pointed out in an earlier chapter, been seriously questioned by the originators of the earliest Harvard film course (Dearborn and Anderson, 1937; Anderson and Dearborn, 1952). Doubts about their value have also been expressed by Perry (1959) who, jointly with Whitlock, devised the later series of Harvard films (Perry and Whitlock, 1948a and b). It is now generally accepted that the films are mainly motivational, a point made a number of years ago by Perry himself and by Hodgins (1971) in explaining the continued use of film pacing at Harvard. Webster (1964), writing up his own course, comments that he is uncertain about the intrinsic value of films, but he considers they provide 'a source of discussion and entertainment and a valuable aid to group cohesion' (p. 46). The only other piece of mechanical equipment in common use in British courses, is the metronome used by Buzan in the College of Advanced Reading course at Sussex (Watts and Buzan, 1973) in an attempt to train the eyes to read at speeds far in excess of normal.

A characteristic of the commercial courses is their expectation of a large increase in the student's speed during the early exercises. Other courses predict more gradual change. The exercises used on these other courses are usually specially prepared short passages of 500 – 1200 words, which are followed by comprehension questions. The commercial concerns, on the other hand, often make use of ordinary texts, a training method sometimes described as paperback scanning (Berger, 1970). With this method, oral recall, subjective assessment or a few notes are accepted as evidence of comprehension. Pacing on the commercial courses is often achieved by using one's own hand or finger as a pacing device on an ordinary text. The ready availability of this instrument permits the use of a wider range and a larger amount of material for paced practice than do the courses which use films as pacers. Some refinements on hand pacing involve moving the hand or finger so that various shapes are traced on the page. By following this procedure it is claimed that non-sequential reading habits develop and one might agree that this kind of exercise appears somewhat more closely related to normal reading than does the reading of phrases projected sequentially onto a screen.

In courses such as those of Wainwright (1967, 1969) the reader paces himself, although films are sometimes used. As in other courses, the reader is advised to read in phrases rather than in words or letters. What control a reader has over what he sees and processes in one fixation is uncertain, but, in general, courses inform the student that he may increase his reading speed by reducing the time spent per fixation while increasing the amount seen per fixation. Buzan (1974) also claims to enable students to utilize peripheral vision. The amount and accuracy of theoretical exposition varies from course to course but poor visual behaviour and sub-vocalization are blamed by most of the courses for 'poor' initial performance of students. Sub-vocalization may be difficult to eliminate, since it appears to be involuntary and may well accompany most adult reading and many types of thinking (*see* Chapter 3). Nonetheless, students are encouraged to avoid the habit, usually on the grounds that sub-vocalizing forces the reader to keep to the same rate in silent reading as he does in oral reading. This is also doubtful. Buzan advocates occupying the lips with making a commentary on the text as reading proceeds, but other courses seem to offer little constructive advice on the problem, if indeed it is one. The Carborundum course (Gregory, 1966) as offered by the Production Engineering Research Association in April 1968, recommended biting on a pencil but this advice is not usual.

The main emphasis in the training is often on visual aspects of reading. Many courses provide exercises intended to aid rapid recognition. The films are partly intended to serve this function but other means of training have been devised. Sometimes these are in the form of pages with lines drawn down the middle; students are here advised to read either in one fixation per line or half line of text. Sometimes the drills consist of working rapidly through lists of words of increasing length, or through tables of digits or letters in meaningless combinations. In yet others the text is broken up into phrases or short lines so that the student may practice the reading in phrases, which most courses advocate.

A form of visual behaviour which is usually regarded as bad practice, on the grounds that it slows down reading, is improperly described as regression. The term strictly refers to the involuntary regressive eye movements made in reading a text and, since the movements are involuntary, the reader has, by definition, no control over them. In the courses the term regression is extended to include any looking back over a text. Clearly there are occasions when looking back at a text is deliberate or, at least, conscious, and advice to avoid this type of regression will be easier to follow than the advice about involuntary behaviour. The value of the advice for reading outside the reading tasks in the courses is another question, since it is sometimes essential to look back in order to understand well enough to read on.

Apart from attempting to increase reading by the aid of practice, pacing and advice of the type mentioned, some courses also claim to teach skimming, a term which appears to be used for various activities and which is discussed more fully in the next chapter. On the film-aided courses the term is taken to mean reading in excess of six hundred words per minute. Wainwright (1968) also appears to regard skimming as fast reading. The commercial concerns, on the other hand, do not generally differentiate fast reading from skimming, preferring to use the term reading for all speeds. Buzan, however, does make a distinction in his book (Buzan, 1971), arguing that the very fast reading he develops is distinct from skimming.

The courses do not examine the uses of skimming in any depth but tend to regard it simply as a skill which is of general use. Wainwright, however, refers to the SQ3R sequence (Robinson, 1946) in which skimming is used for initial survey and for review of study reading material. (See Chapter 5 for information on this and similar strategies.) Indeed, in the second half of his published course (Wainwright, 1968) the exercises are all to be previewed before reading. The original American course in Evelyn Wood's Reading Dynamics made widespread use of previewing as an aid to rapid reading. This use of previewing was noted by Spache (1962) who maintained that the high speeds of reading claimed for students on the Evelyn Wood courses were in part due to the five-minute preview which was allowed to precede the reading of some texts. Dynamic Reading and Advanced Reading, while subscribing neither to the term skimming in connection with fast reading nor to the SQ3R approach for study, nonetheless encourage rapid previewing and reviewing of materials. Multiple reading of study material was recommended by Dynamic Reading and the 'Buzan Study Technique' which was used by the College of Advanced Reading appears to be an extension of this multiple reading approach.

None of the courses is very clear about relating speed of reading to the purpose for which the reading is done. Although many do recognize that different reading tasks require different approaches, no great prominence is given to training in a variety of different approaches or to identifying their appropriateness in situations outside the course. The commercial concerns differentiate between a fast speed for general reading and a study reading speed, while Wainwright follows Fry (1963a) in suggesting three speeds, (study, average and skimming) and likens them to car gears. The speeds are suggested as appropriate for certain kinds of task (e.g. slow for study reading) but no distinction is made between the reader's purpose and the type of reading material, it being implied that certain purposes are always inherent in certain texts. The Carborundum course and the Harvard course seem to pay little attention to varying rate according to subject matter and purpose, although the existence of such variations is recognized. Indeed, for the revised version of the Carborundum course (i.e. the version referred to so far) the subject matter of the practice material was deliberately changed so that all passages were biographies; reviewing the new course, Wellens (1966) notes that criticisms had been made of the earlier Carborundum course, (*Speed up your Reading*, Bayley, 1960) on the grounds that there were fluctuations in difficulty owing to the type of subject matter used.

Advice is sometimes given on a number of other matters relating to reading which have not so far been mentioned. For example, many courses recommend having a check-up at the opticians; others make mention of topics such as lighting and posture. The College of Advanced Reading gave advice and practice on note-taking and on a variety of other matters including the appreciation of literature, typography, preparing essays and speeches, and taking examinations.

The tutored courses differ according to the type of equipment and pacing used and according to the type of material used for practice. The advice given differs in scope, but certain advice (e.g. to read more per fixation and to avoid regression and sub-vocalization) seems to be common to all the courses. The emphasis overall is on increasing reading speed rather than varying it according to text and purpose, and the uses of various reading skills and strategies are not examined fully, if at all. No attempt is normally made to improve comprehension, and the type of comprehension test used in the practice exercises varies from course to course.

Method used in published courses

From the point of view of the student the published courses differ in some important ways from the tutored courses. For example, the student taking a published course is unaffected by the interaction between members of the group and is denied the pacing effect of group practice. He is also considerably less influenced by the personality of the tutor who cannot, of course, respond to the student. Owing to their elusive nature, these factors have necessarily been neglected in examining the tutored courses. With the published courses, on the other hand, it is much easier to identify factors which might operate on the student since the stimulus material is readily available for examination.

The published courses appear to be only slightly modified for home study and are often little more than rewritten versions of tutored courses. The regular use of the second person to address the reader betrays the origins of certain courses and causes them to read in parts rather like lectures or talks. However, this similarity between the content and design of the two types of course has certain advantages, since one may make more specific comment on some of the matters already raised in the previous section while at the same time arguing reasonably that much of what is true for published courses is also true for tutored courses.

The published courses consist of books ranging in length from under eighty pages (Reading Laboratory Inc., 1971) to over eight hundred pages, in two volumes (Richaudeau and Gauquelin, 1966). Most of the books contain information by the author and exercises on which the reader may practise reading continuous prose. The exercises are followed by questions normally to be answered without reference back to the text. The questions are usually of the multiple-choice or forced-choice type, but may be free-response, or a mixture of free-response and forced-choice. A few courses ask for a summary of some of the passages read. Questions are almost always given after reading, although some hint as to the type of questions to be asked is given in a small number of courses. The two courses (Reading Laboratory Inc., 1971; Weber and Schatte, 1972) which contain no exercises in reading continuous prose, nevertheless contain pre-tests in the same form as the exercises described above. The courses by Mares (1964) and by Weber and Schatte are the only ones examined with no post-test; all the other courses examined have both pre- and post-tests of some kind.

A very large number of the courses have regular tests or exercises which are claimed to provide the reader with feedback on his performance. Dudley (1964) presents the rationale for this procedure clearly when he states that practice without information on how well one is doing is not very effective. The truth of this view is not in doubt but the reliability of the feedback provided by many speed reading tests is suspect.

Apart from exercises in reading continuous prose, some books contain exercises intended to widen the eye-span, reduce fixation time, prevent regression or develop desirable kinds of visual behaviour. Some books completely ignore this kind of exercise; de Leeuw and de Leeuw (1965) indeed, devote several pages in their book to explaining its irrelevance. Webster (1964) on the other hand, considers that the visual exercises may have some value and gives reasons for his views, unlike many authors who seem to include such exercises for no better reason than that other courses contain them. The original influence is probably Pitkin's early course (Pitkin, 1929) which contained a number of eye-span exercises.

Some of the exercises are attempts to reproduce the effect of a tachistoscope (i.e. a device for exposing visual images for a short predetermined period). Two courses sold by mail order contain a device described as a near point tachistoscope, and one course (Ott, 1970) contains a piece of plastic which is placed over a word, compressed and then allowed to flick free. The idea is that the word at the top of the compressed plastic can only be seen for a short time once the hand pressure on the plastic is released. Most courses which subscribe to a concern with discontinuous word recognition at speed merely suggest that the reader should cut a hole in a card so that when the card moves the words in a text can only be seen for a short time.

In the published courses it is easy enough to devise methods which appear superficially to produce an effect similar to tachistoscopic presentation of words and phrases. Pitkin used the technique of printing one isolated phrase per page; the reader is to enlist the help of an assistant who turns the pages so that the reader receives only a fleeting view of the phrases. Possibly because of the expense involved in printing one phrase per page, it is more usual for drills of this kind to be based on several words or phrases printed on each page. Sometimes the pages are specially arranged so that a triangle or similar figure of words and phrases of gradually increasing length appears on the page, as in the German and many of the American courses.

The American courses often provide exercises in sense matching at speed in addition to exercises which involve rapid visual recognition; accordingly a number of them contain lists of words with, to the right of each listed word, a group of about five words, one of which is similar in meaning to the word on the list. The task is to underline the correct synonyms as rapidly as possible. The justification for the inclusion of these exercises seems to be that a good vocabulary is important for reading, which is not disputed, and that these exercises extend vocabulary. However, it is hard to see how this extension can come about, since the exercises appear to be testing existing ability. More commonly, courses aim to extend vocabulary by providing lists of prefixes and affixes to be learnt. A few courses, especially those of American origin, also deal with analysis of paragraphs and provide exercises in finding the topic sentence or main idea.

Those British courses which are concerned with eye-movement training sometimes require the reader to prepare his own materials from instructions given by the author. Dudley (1964) for instance, suggests that the reader should draw a pencil line down from the middle of some of his pages. Taking the pencil line as the centre of the fixation, the student is often advised to read a whole line at a time. Bayley (1957) is content merely to recommend certain fixation patterns appropriate to reading a

line rapidly, but Mares (1964) gives a few exercises of the triangle type, together with some in which the text is divided into phrases, for 'phrase-reading'. Buzan (1971) gives a number of exercises in reading digits which form numbers of gradually increasing length. This is not, however, a major feature of his 'advanced reading techniques'. For developing these, he advocates the use of the hand as a pacer for the eyes and the use of 'vertical vision' to permit a larger area of focus as a prelude to 'the large-print-area reading method'. This latter method is not treated in Buzan's published course.

The European courses undoubtedly pay the greatest attention to eye-movement practice. Richaudeau and Gauquelin (1966) devote over a hundred pages to various *gammes* or exercises, in addition to other exercises in the text. Ott's (1970) book is dominated by a variety of ingenious exercises; some involve following lines around a page but these and others seem to have rather little relevance even to word recognition. Weber and Schatte (1972) also devote many of their pages to eye training with isolated words and, in addition, have pages marked with light grey lines in various shapes. One page, for example, has its text covered in a large grey letter S which it is intended the reader's eyes should follow.

The value of these exercises and their relevance to reading continuous prose is in doubt, as some courses seem to indicate by omitting them. Even so, it is not possible to find a course which does not make some reference to eye-movements. All suggest that visual behaviour requires to be altered; it is rather the means of change which is in dispute and some courses rely much more heavily on practice in continuous prose reading, within the course and outside it, than do others.

Apart from some concern with visual behaviour many of the courses recommend that sub-vocalization can be avoided. For some writers (e.g. Bayley, 1957; Buzan, 1971; Ott, 1970; Richaudeau and Gauquelin, 1966; and Dudley, 1964) the 'sound barrier' is the main cause of reading problems, while others, notably de Leeuw and de Leeuw (1965) doubt whether sub-vocalization is either detrimental or avoidable. Fry (1963a) regards it as a major fault among overseas students, but neither Harris (1966) nor Yorkey (1970) mentions it in this connection. Indeed apart from Fry, Pitkin (1929) is the only American author among those surveyed who gives prominence to the topic. Pitkin's early remarks, while in accord with evidence recently reviewed by Conrad (1972), are quite contradictory to the assumptions of the many courses which regard sub-vocalization as both harmful and remediable.

Despite some differences in the scope of their aim and in their coverage of topics, the differences between the published courses are not on central issues, but are rather in matters of emphasis, length and format. One might expect, for example, that there would be some essential differences in courses according to the audience for which they were originally devised and are still loosely intended. The differences which do occur are, however, largely peripheral. Thus the American courses tend to be longer and to contain a wider variety of exercises, presumably because it is anticipated that they may be used as a basis for a full course in compulsory classes. The European courses, on the other hand, are rarely based on courses devised for use as a compulsory part of college or university study and tend to be shorter and to cover fewer topics.

One obvious difference between the published courses, however, is in their typographical design and layout. A comparison between two of the European courses is revealing. Richaudeau and Gauquelin (1966) published their course in two large volumes, using good quality white paper and with text printed in well spaced conventional book type. Weber and Schatte (1972), on the other hand, use double columns of close set bold type on greyish paper for their slim volume. Interestingly both writers draw attention to typography and layout and state that theirs is based on legibility researches, at the Universities of Lille and Hamburg respectively.

Other relatively minor differences between courses are, like their major assumptions, often justified by an appeal to research. Unfortunately the sources of information are rarely given and there are fewer books with a bibliography than without one among the published courses surveyed. Precise details of the sources, even of quotations, are rarely given and this makes for difficulties in judging the soundness of some of the assumptions and assertions which are made.

Conclusion and summary

Among the courses examined one is more impressed by the similarities than by the differences. In both the tutored and the published courses there is a common concern with increasing speed of reading while maintaining the level of measured comprehension. Despite the broader aims of some courses, this concern assumes prominence through the regular practice in reading continuous prose at speed. Some courses aim for a greater change in speed than others, but the student is advised in all the courses to increase his speed. This statement of behavioural objectives in terms of speed typifies the courses examined here and it distinguishes them from courses such as those held at Brunel and Leeds Universities which will be referred to in the next chapter. There the emphasis was on developing greater awareness of the appropriateness of different reading techniques for various tasks and purposes.

It has been noted that there are undoubtedly factors operating within a tutored course which cannot operate in a published course. With regard to method, however, the common use of regular timed exercises is more important than differences over the undesirability of sub-vocalization or the disagreement about the use of eye-training exercises. The shared theoretical basis of most of the courses, and the agreement about the areas in which an adult should change his behaviour in order to become a better reader, are the more surprising when one considers the variety of date and countries of origin of the courses referred to here.

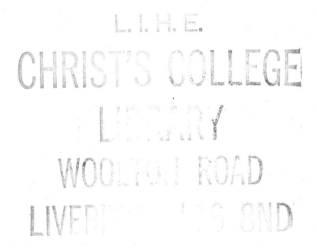

5

An Approach to Developing Efficiency in Silent Reading

The similarities noted between speed reading courses derive from their common source in the psychological researches of the early years of this century and the experiments in American schools in the 1920s. Unfortunately, it appears that many devisers of courses have been content to copy each other's methods rather than take account of the needs of those for whom the courses are intended. As already suggested, it is doubtful whether the jargon and hardware used in many speed reading courses are necessary or helpful and the theoretical basis of the courses is suspect. Nevertheless, it does appear that the courses appeal to a real need for help with silent reading, even if they cannot really satisfy this need.

It has been implied already that there must be considerable doubts about the desirability of using an unmodified speed reading course with schoolchildren or with students. Although some children (and adults) may sometimes read unnecessarily slowly, there may well be stages in reading development in which practice in the rapid silent reading of a text is either impossible or unhelpful. Also the value of speed of reading for its own sake is questionable. 'Whom are they fleeing from, these running readers?' asked I. A. Richards and concluded that it must be 'themselves' (Richards, 1943 p. 42). Writing about the use of speed reading courses with particular reference to the work of the British Council overseas, MacMillan (1965) has also queried the desirability of placing such great emphasis on speed, claiming that the value of reading as a suitable context for thought was in danger of being overlooked. Vernon (1931) reviewed early work in speed reading and then, as later, questioned its value and importance for most readers (*cf* Vernon, 1969).

In devising courses for use with University students at Brunel

University, Thomas and Harri-Augstein (1976) have been less concerned with speed than with strategy and have stressed the importance of reading in different ways for different purposes. In the United States too and especially during the past ten or fifteen years the concern with speed reading has diminished, at least relatively. Writers have begun to stress the importance of purpose in reading and a number of researchers have attempted to construct tests of flexibility in reading. Rankin (1974) reviews some of this work and shows that it has not been entirely successful. Yet, as Farr (1969) has pointed out in a critical review of standardized reading tests, if the apparent ease of measuring speed in reading is illusory it is hardly surprising that measurement of flexibility (i.e. varying rate according to difficulty and purpose) presents problems.

More recently, therefore, the appeal of speed reading has diminished and yet other approaches to the teaching of silent reading have not yet become firmly established. Given this situation the writer had to devise a course for students at the University of Leeds. This involved thinking carefully about the objectives of a course in reading efficiency, devising methods for teaching such a course and finally finding ways of evaluating the course. Because it is the principles on which the course was based (rather than its detail) which are likely to be useful, the fullest attention is given here to setting out the thinking underlying it. Some of the principles, at least, are applicable to attempts to help secondary school children develop their reading. However, the teaching of silent reading in schools is dealt with more fully in the next chapter.

Efficiency and purpose in reading

The adult reader normally reads in order to achieve certain purposes, whereas in the development of reading fluency the purpose for reading may often not be very clear. In order to achieve his purposes the adult will use a variety of appropriate reading styles, whereas at the stage of fluency the tendency will be to read straight through a text in a fairly even-paced manner, using an approach which was designated aural reading in Chapter 2, where it was argued that fluent reading is akin to listening. Speed reading courses often encourage rapid reading straight through a text and may, therefore, encourage reading of an aural type rather than help develop the strategies used in true silent reading by efficient readers.

Efficiency in mechanics refers to the ratio between effort expended and useful work done. The more near perfect the ratio, the more efficient is the machine. The term efficiency has been similarly used in psychological research (see e.g. Ryan, 1947) but the human organism, especially when performing complex tasks, does not lend itself so readily as a machine to the assessment of its efficiency. There are particular problems in the study of reading since both the input (effort expended) and output (useful work done) are difficult to measure. We shall return to these difficulties in Chapters 7 and 8; but the concept of efficiency is a useful one despite the problems of measurement, for it draws attention to the goal-directed nature of adult reading and highlights the importance of purpose. Defining one's purpose is of particular importance in independent study and it is for this reason it was emphasized in the course for students at the University of Leeds. Some observations made during the development and evaluation of the course supported the suspicion that it was in the area of defining one's purpose and task and choosing the appropriate reading strategy that the difficulties of many students lay. Other studies suggested that this was also true of sixth formers and of middle schoolchildren, although some of the children may also have had some problems with reading fluently (see Pugh, 1976; Neville and Pugh, 1975c, 1977).

Many writers on reading, including many of the authors of speed reading courses, have stated that reading should be regarded as a purposeful activity. Unfortunately few have gone beyond this bald assertion which is not particularly helpful as it stands, unless the possible purposes for reading are generally understood. Some researchers in the United States have attempted to be more explicit. Smith (1972) differentiates between primary purposes (i.e. the ultimate basic purposes for which people read) and secondary purposes on which she concentrates. These secondary purposes appear rather close to the comprehension skills or reading skills which American tests attempt to measure (see especially Chapters 7 and 8) but this is perhaps necessarily so, since primary purposes are not easily observed whereas secondary purposes, as used here, seem to mean mainly testable purposes. However, Smith reports a transfer of the use of skills learnt by children in her study of textbook materials.

Farnes (1973), who had formerly been concerned with reading courses for undergraduates at Brunel University, attempts to define purpose in reading in the context of the Open University's *Reading Development* course. He distinguishes between what he calls life purposes, role purposes and task purposes and concludes that it is task purposes which must mainly concern the teacher of reading. Both Farnes and Smith suggest that skill in achieving task purposes, or secondary purposes can be improved by practice in answering questions which define the purpose for the reader. As noted earlier West (1926) had also paid considerable attention to the role of questioning in developing different styles of reading.

Some criticism has been made of the questioning approach by Steinacher (1971) who argues that teachers were not so much improving children's reading ability by the use of questions, as specifying more clearly to the children the task which was to be done. However, one can also argue that the use of questions to set purposes may well give both experience and insight which will help in the development of the different styles and strategies which can be used in reading. The question of whether any change occurs in reading ability is perhaps better left, in view of the debate about what is meant by basic ability. Nevertheless it is important to recognize the very real danger to which Steinacher refers of the aims of the teaching being lost in a series of arid exercises.

Reading styles

There is no accepted taxonomy of the skills used by adult readers, and even where terminology is available there is confusion over its use. Thus, for example, the terms skimming and scanning are often used interchangeably in the American literature. Whether the term skill should be used for different kinds of adult reading is also questionable. Lunzer (1976) rightly draws attention to the imprecise and confusing uses of the term in the study of reading. Hence the term *style* is used here for the different kinds of reading which were identified from introspection and from observing readers taking the *Techniques for Effective Reading* course at the University of Leeds, or doing tasks which were monitored on closed circuit television. The five major styles which were identified are scanning; search reading; skimming; receptive reading; and responsive reading. The styles certainly merge with each other, and any one task may well contain elements of more than one style. Nevertheless, it is clearer for the present to examine the styles in their 'pure' form.

Scanning is used within a text to locate a specific symbol or group of symbols (such as a particular phrase, formula, name or date). The reader knows what the symbol or group of symbols looks like and, therefore, he also knows when he has located what he is seeking. In his visual activity the reader exhibits a mixture of rapid inspection of the text with an occasional closer inspection. He need not read line by line and may well, in a book, disregard the author's sequencing. It is reasonable to assume that very little information is processed for long-term retention or even for immediate understanding, since the task is really one of finding a match between what is sought and what is given in the text. A total mismatch may be rapidly rejected, while a near match will be examined more carefully.

Search reading is a more demanding mental activity since here the reader is attempting to locate information on a topic when he is not certain of the precise form in which the information will appear. He may, to take an example given by a student, be trying to find and collect information on the topic of the Inquisition in England. If, as in this example, the book is about the Inquisition in Europe he will need to inspect carefully those parts where the word 'England' appears in conjunction with the word 'Inquisition'. He will also, however, need to bear in mind that words such as the name of any English town or county or a generic term such as 'Britain' or 'United Kingdom' may also be a clue to locating relevant information. Similarly the Inquisition may be described as the 'Holy Office' or some other variant may be used. One way in which search reading differs from scanning, therefore, is that the reader is not pursuing a simple visual matching task, but rather needs to remain alert to various words in a similar semantic field to the topic in which he is interested. It is true that the visual activity involved is similar to scanning in many ways. However, the periods of close attention to the text tend to be more frequent and of longer duration and, since information is more deeply embedded in the text, there is more observance of the way in which the author structures his subject matter and, hence, the linearity and sequencing. Information about the structure of the text may be used to assist in the search but will not be usefully remembered in the long term, for the intention is only to learn the information which is relevant to the original topic.

Skimming is visually similar to search reading in that periods of close inspection of the text occur during an overall rapid inspection. Here, however, the author's sequence (but not his linearity) is better observed, since the reader is no longer seeking predetermined information. Rather he is attempting to use the author's structure for one of a number of reasons. To counter the view that skimming is used to obtain a rough impression of a text, it is most important to stress that skimming may be used as a process operation, whereby the reader is enabled to make an informed decision on how (if at all) and for what purpose he will approach the text during a subsequent encounter. Skimming may, indeed, also be used to obtain an overall impression of features of a text. For example, it may be used to glean surface information, to check on a writer's tone, or to discover how a writer structures a chapter. Related to discovering the structure is a further use of skimming, where the reader seeks 'advance organization' of what he is subsequently to learn in detail. Ausubel (1968) and many others have stressed the importance of cognitive organization for learning; through skimming, the reader may be able to provide his own organization without needing a teacher or author to do it for him. Finally, an important use of skimming is in reviewing and revising what has been read, so that the learning may be consolidated. Since skimming is used for so many purposes, it is difficult to make inferences about the mental activity which accompanies it. It is clear, however, that in all cases the reader is concerned with the way in which the author presents his information and that, whatever his purpose in skimming, the reader will be storing some information in a form similar to that in which the author structures his text. This means that skimming is a more complex task than scanning or search reading, for it requires the reader to organize and remember some of the information which the author provides, rather than simply to locate it.

Receptive reading is used when one wishes to discover accurately what an author seeks to convey. The reader is much more willing to be directed by the author than in the styles described so far, for he wishes to obtain what I. A. Richards (1929) has called 'the plain sense'. In other words, the reader allows the author his say, without on the one hand skimming or omitting sections or, on the other hand, indulging in a great deal of reflective thought. The visual behaviour which accompanies this kind of reading is similar to that obtained from photographic records of eye-movements. The reader observes the author's sequence and follows along the printer's lines, with close attention to small units in the visual display. Occasionally there may be a glance back at the text but the progression is mainly even and in a forward direction. The mental activity involves organizing and remembering the essence of what is read, but is not punctuated by long periods devoted to thinking prompted by the text.

In the fifth style, responsive reading, the reader may well spend considerable periods with little attention to the text. His purpose here is to use what the author conveys as a prompt to reflective or creative thought. It is this kind of reading and thinking to which MacMillan (1965) seems to refer when he argues that the value of reading in providing a suitable context for thinking is sometimes ignored in courses which emphasise speed of reading.

Strategic use of styles

The styles of reading given in the previous section are unlikely to be used alone, but rather will be used in conjunction with each other in a strategic approach to reading. Skimming, for example, is often used for making decisions on how to approach texts. Search reading or scanning will often result in receptive reading of certain parts of a text. The grounds upon which readers choose their strategies are not well understood since they have not been fully investigated. However, some observations and records have been made of the ways in which adults and students use texts for various reading purposes. Fuller details of the methods used for these studies are given in Chapter 8, but both the Brunel

University studies (Thomas and Harri-Augstein, 1976) and those with which the writer has been concerned, indicate that readers do vary their style of reading according to what they are trying to achieve when using a text.

Studies carried out in connection with the *Techniques for Effective Reading* course at Leeds were mainly concerned with the use of books for locating information. Questions which set the reading purpose were given to the student before he opened the book and these questions were designed to elicit certain styles of reading. Here the strategy necessary for efficient use of texts involved using guides to the structure of a book such as the index, table of contents, section headings, whereas the studies at Brunel were mainly concerned with strategy for studying a chapter or other relatively short text.

Some writers have advocated strategies for reading books for study. Perhaps the best known of these is Robinson's SQ3R method, which is recommended in various forms in many speed reading courses. This method (Robinson, 1946) involves the student in surveying, questioning, reading, reviewing and reciting. A multiple reading approach is also recommended and described by the de Leeuws (de Leeuw and de Leeuw, 1965). Buzan (1971) also advocates a multiple reading approach, as was noted in Chapter 4.

The basis for these prescriptions and recommendations is not always well established and the study approach recommended often seems to be a misfit in speed reading courses. For the course at Leeds a chart was drawn up to show the ways in which the various reading styles could be used to approach books strategically for various purposes. Within the course, the following algorithmic flow chart was used to encourage students to make decisions about books in a short period, but it also served to indicate how the styles which had been identified could be used in conjunction with each other.

The course did not go beyond the level of using a book, although there may well be a need, even for students at a university, to be given help in using libraries, carrying out information searches, and collating and organizing information. Certainly a study by Mann (1973) among students at Sheffield University indicated that many students did not use libraries and that few appeared to know how to do so. However, Mann

Flow chart showing the flexible approach to book use

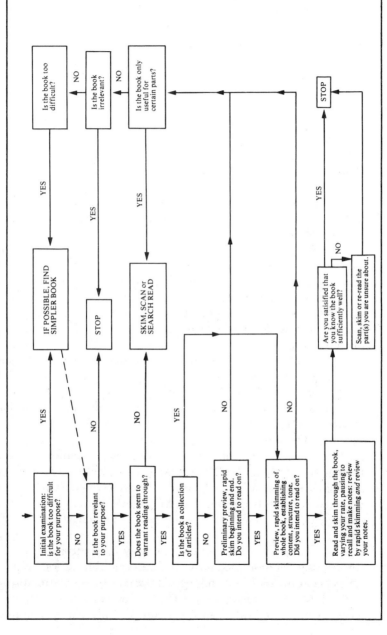

concluded (and probably rightly,) that it is the student's specialist subject tutor who can help most in this area.

The Techniques for Effective Reading course

The *Techniques for Effective Reading* course was available to students and staff at the University of Leeds from 1971 to 1974. Courses were also given for extra-mural students. Attendance was entirely voluntary and of necessity any group would contain members of various departments and faculties. Typically a course consisted of eight meetings of $1\frac{1}{4}$ hours, held at weekly intervals.

The main objective was to enable students to read more efficiently and flexibly. More specific objectives were:

1 to enable students to use a variety of reading styles and strategies

2 to enable students to clarify, as far as possible, their own reading purposes when they encountered a text

3 to help students adopt the appropriate styles and strategies for achieving their purposes

Also, because of the effect of physical conditions on reading (see Carmichael and Dearborn, 1948; Tinker, 1965) a further objective was:

4 to enable students to recognize external physical conditions which affect efficiency

Each meeting contained some reading practice, a talk by the tutor, group discussion and advice for practising or applying the approaches to reading which had been dealt with at that meeting. The talks covered topics such as speed and flexibility in reading; comprehension; reading purposes; memory; note-taking and fatigue; and conditions for effective reading. A summary of these talks was given in a booklet which each student received at the beginning of the course. The booklet also contained other information, such as the flow chart referred to earlier (p. 57).

As in the speed reading courses, however, it seems likely that the reading exercises taken by students would have a considerable effect on what they understood the course to be attempting to teach them. At the first meeting, tests of two styles of reading were given, namely receptive reading and search reading.

Equivalent forms of these tests had been devised (*see* Pugh 1974 for full details) but the intercorrelations between scores on these equivalent forms were not as high as would be required for tests for individual assessment. However, one main purpose of using these tests was to alert students to the existence of two distinct styles of silent reading, and a secondary purpose was to provide evaluation of group performance.

For the next two or three meetings, advantage was taken of one of the weaknesses of speed reading courses. Such factors as familiarity with the type of exercise used and with the purpose of reading, as indicated by questions given after reading, were used to good effect in order to help students who could not read quickly to obtain some experience of doing so.

However, after students were found to be reading considerably more quickly on this kind of task, and it was revealed to them that they had made the kind of gains which they might expect from a speed reading course, the reasons for their apparent success were explained. Thus it was pointed out that more rapid reading is possible once the purpose of reading is established and where the nature of the task is known. However, it was also noted that rapid reading is often more akin to skimming than to receptive reading.

At this point in the course, exercises were given in skimming to determine the structure of a text and for surface information. From here on, however, the practice was mainly intended to provide experience of reading styles leading to discussion and application of them. It was emphasized that the student should not expect to receive accurate feedback on his performance since the difficulties of measuring performance in skimming are even greater than those inherent in attempting to measure performance in receptive reading or search reading. Later meetings were concerned with the clarification of reading styles, with the practice of different strategies and with discussion of them in the context of note-taking, using books for information and study, and lighting and other factors in the physical environment which affect reading efficiency.

Evaluation of the course

At the end of the course parallel forms of the tests given at the first meeting were taken, and some evidence on student's views of the course were obtained by means of an unsigned questionnaire. A questionnaire had also been given at the first meeting to establish, among other things, what students hoped to gain from the course. These were the only methods of evaluation used within the course. However, a small controlled study was made (partly using a method involving video-tape recording described in Chapter 8) to compare a sample of students who had completed the course with, as a control group, a similar sample who intended to do so, but had not yet been able to take up a place. Those who had completed the course were also interviewed.

The results from evaluation within the course showed that students who completed a course worked significantly more quickly at the end than at the beginning, when compared on comparable tests of search reading and receptive reading. However, as with speed reading courses, these results can to some extent be explained in terms of familiarity with the task and the degree of real improvement is hard to gauge. Just over 50 per cent of those who enrolled completed a course. Questionnaires and interviews suggested that most of these students considered that they had benefitted from attending. Most students in their questionnaire responses instanced situations or tasks where what they had learned in the course had proved useful. There was a very wide range of responses to the question which asked what aspect of the course had been most useful, although skimming was the style considered to be most valuable.

The controlled study, carried out with twenty-one first year students in an experimental group and a similar number in a matched control group revealed that the experimental subjects were no quicker in using books for locating information than the control subjects, but that the experimental group tended to be more accurate.

Evaluation poses problems because of the lack of satisfactory tests to give a measure of the full effects of a course. For this reason Maxwell (1971) has argued that it is important to assess the effect of a course on the academic performance of those who have taken it. In doing this care needs to be taken to control for the possibility that those who choose to take a course are better motivated to study than those who choose not to take one. Account was taken of this possibility in the evaluation just mentioned, as it was in a study at an Australian university

(Francis, Collins and Cassel, 1973) designed to assess the effects of taking a speed reading course on the academic performance of students on an Introduction to Psychology course. They also studied a group who volunteered for the speed reading course but did not in fact take it. Here, it was found that neither volunteering for a course, nor actually taking a course had any impact upon academic grades, although other studies cited by these researchers had found the contrary to be the case.

With the Leeds course it was not possible to assess effects upon academic performance since students came from so many different departments. In this kind of situation one reaction to the problems of evaluation is to unduly restrict the course to narrow objectives so that only what appears easily measurable is taught. As Maxwell (1971) suggests, there may be pressure in some colleges and universities to do this in order to have presentable results for such administrative purposes as the renewal of a grant to permit courses to continue. Fortunately, the course at Leeds was free of pressures of this kind.

Perhaps a more serious difficulty is that tests need to be highly reliable if they are to provide a student with feedback from which he learns. (Many discussions of the role of feedback and knowledge of results in learning are available: *see* e.g. Holding, 1965). If a student modifies his behaviour as a result of misleading feedback, he may well modify in the wrong direction. This is a strong argument against speed reading courses, but it cannot be used to suggest that the range of reading styles which can be taught must be limited to what can be measured with accuracy. Nevertheless, serious account must be taken of these measurement problems and for this reason students taking the course at the University of Leeds were alerted to the difficulties in assessing their performance and were encouraged to pay at least as much attention to the reasons for the results they achieved as to the results themselves.

Conclusion and summary

This chapter has suggested that there are several styles of reading used by efficient readers. The styles have been delineated and an account given of an attempt to encourage students to use these styles as part of a strategic approach to reading. The importance

of purpose in reading has also been emphasized. The approach taken in speed reading courses is, it has been argued, too narrow and, indeed, the results from tests used in these courses are misleading both for the student who seeks feedback and to those concerned with evaluating speed reading courses. The measurement of the styles of reading given, and especially of their strategic use, also poses problems but these should not be allowed to cause an undue restriction on what is regarded, or taught, as good silent reading behaviour.

More positively, suggestions have been given for how a course in reading efficiency might be organized, and this may provide some ideas for those who wish to teach silent reading in schools. However, the question as to who should teach such courses in schools or universities is an open one. Whether the subject specialist should concern himself with how his students learn in his own subject or whether there is room for courses devoted to reading and study skills requires careful consideration. However, as is argued in the next chapter, unless this issue is resolved there is a danger that developing efficiency in reading will fail to be regarded as the responsibility of anyone teaching beyond the primary school.

6

Silent Reading in Schools—
some Considerations and Suggestions

Questions have already been raised on the role of schools in the development of silent reading, and some suggestions relevant to its teaching have been made. The important distinction has been established between the development of fluency, dealt with briefly in Chapter 3, and the development of true silent reading skills. Also it has been suggested that approaches based on speed reading are unlikely to be helpful unless used cautiously since they do not appear to be very effective for developing fluency and they distract attention from the variety of styles related to purpose which are used in effective adult reading.

A number of important questions remain. These centre on what should be taught in secondary schools and at what stage, who should be responsible for the teaching, and what methods might be used. Unfortunately these are not really distinct questions, for the answer to one question dictates the possible answers to the next. Yet one cannot give definitive answers since, because of the neglect of silent reading in secondary education, there is insufficient experience or evidence to provide a basis for sound prescription.

Two other considerations affect this discussion. One is the broad question of the relevance of the school curriculum in general to the needs of children when they leave school. This is very contentious since it involves clarification of the needs of children beyond school. The other is complementary, in view of the resistance among some teachers of English to a needs-based curriculum, and concerns the role of the English teacher in teaching reading in secondary schools.

Who should be responsible for the teaching of silent reading?

Ultimately, of course, the headteacher is responsible for the curriculum in British schools, although he may be guided by local authority advisers and influenced by the external examination system. However, the headteacher obviously depends to a considerable extent upon the enthusiasm, aptitude and training of his staff particularly in implementing new or unusual work. One problem in attempting to initiate or develop work in silent reading will be the lack of experience of such teaching among his staff and the low status which tends to be accorded to skill teaching.

In the eyes of many of his colleagues, the teacher of English is the person to whom one looks for the development of skills related to literacy. However, the history of the teaching of English in Britain (see Shayer, 1972; Mathieson, 1975) shows that attention has been increasingly directed towards the study of literature, the development of creativity and the nurturing of personal response. The lack of concern for skill, if not its positive neglect, may result from a rejection of the approach based on stereotyped exercises which were favoured in the last century. This reaction is understandable, although such an approach has persisted, at least until relatively recently, in many text-books for GCE and other public examinations. Equally understandable is the desire to teach literature, not only because that is what many teachers of English are best equipped by their own training to teach, but also because the study of literature can give some coherence and substance to what can otherwise become an extremely fragmented subject.

It is unfortunate, nevertheless, that less attention has been paid by writers on English teaching to the activity of reading, leaving aside oral reading, than to the development of taste and discrimination and the provision of opportunity to gain some familiarity with literature (see e.g. D'Arcy, 1973, for a review). None of this has been helped by the over-riding concern of most twentieth-century literary critics with normative criticism, to use a term applied by Daiches (1956) in his *Critical Approaches to Literature*. Many literary critics who have concerned themselves with literature in education have been keen to persuade others of the merits of their selection of authors, and this can be seen even in those books which appear from their titles to consider reading as a behaviour. Thus Ezra Pound's *ABC of Reading* (1934) and Quiller-Couch's *On the Art of Reading* (1920) both relate to what books should be read rather than to how they should be read. It is true that the tradition of practical criticism arising from I. A. Richards and F. R. Leavis does pay considerable attention to how the reading should be done, but it will be noted that the purpose of the reading is to evaluate and the method is close scrutiny of the author's text.

These emphases may well be valid and important, and one can certainly see what gave rise to them, given the low status of English literature as a subject for study in schools and universities at the turn of the century. However, the point being made here is that this type or style of reading and evaluation does not constitute a major part of reading behaviour outside school. Also as noted elsewhere, (*see* Chapters 1 and 7 especially for references and fuller discussion) the approaches used by English teachers (and one cannot safely generalize about what these approaches may be) do not appear to give rise to appreciable enjoyment of the books used in school. Nor, it appears, do they lead to a desire among children to read much after leaving school.

One cause of this failure to read beyond school maybe that teachers do not ensure that children are able to read the books they are given. By this is meant that pupils may lack not only the linguistic and reading abilities necessary but also the context for the task, since some literature might appear little related to their own lives. However, for the purpose of developing silent reading, literary reading even if satisfactorily carried out may not be very useful since the mode appropriate to reading most fiction is, in fact, that which has been designated aural reading. This was seen (Chapter 3) as a pre-requisite for silent reading but the teaching of silent reading itself may well appear to be beyond the scope and inclination of many teachers of English.

The problem for teachers of English in accepting a needs-based curriculum is exacerbated by the anti-industrial and anti-commercial tradition in English literary criticism. (*See* e.g. Williams, 1958.) The view of Sampson (1925) that we must not educate children for their jobs but *against* them may seem humane or unrealistic according to one's standpoint. Whether or not it appears outmoded and rooted in social clashes which are now resolved, the view still persists and contrives to make what the teacher of English has to offer seem irrelevant to some important needs of his pupils.

The effect of attitudes mentioned above on emphases in the teaching of English is considerable, but there are undoubtedly exceptions in practice. For example, a writer such as Flower (1966, 1969) has succeeded, though influenced by the traditions described, in considering the needs for which students learn English. However, it may be noted that Flower was concerned with further education and in this sector, as in the teaching of English as a Foreign Language, there appears to be greater awareness of the need to develop skill than among those who write about English in secondary education.

If, as is suggested, many teachers of English are not well equipped to teach silent reading, then who is to do so? The Bullock report (DES, 1975) recommends that all teachers play their part, perhaps with a co-ordinator with special responsibility. The Newbolt report (Board of Education, 1921) also accepted that all teachers have a responsibility for language development. Unfortunately, evidence such as that of Barnes *et al.* (1969), though mainly concerned with the spoken language of teachers in their teaching, gives rise to a suspicion that it would be unrealistic to expect teachers in general to develop a concern for such matters as reading styles and strategies. It is, of course, important to appreciate that all teachers do affect (and possibly hinder as well as help) the development of language skills and of learning techniques in their pupils. Nevertheless, there is an important distinction between this incidental influence and the assumption of primary responsibilty for work in this field.

In reality it seems likely, especially since the Bullock recommendations are not to be supported financially, that in certain schools some enthusiasts will pay attention to silent reading and that many other good teachers will continue to help children develop the reading styles and strategies appropriate for the study of their subjects. Unfortunately, as noted earlier (Chapter 1), the type of reading appropriate to much study in school, where study is often a group activity, will not be very helpful for the development of silent reading for independent study.

There do seem to be grounds, therefore, for emulating universities in this respect and at least experimenting with courses specifically concerned with silent reading for independent study, bearing in mind the warnings in the Bullock report and the problems of transfer of learning from such courses. If this is to happen some teachers, whatever their original specialism, will need to devote some of their time to devising and teaching courses in silent reading.

What should be taught as silent reading in secondary schools?

Clearly schools have an important responsibility for ensuring that children leave with, at very least, a basic level of literacy. This term is not well defined but may be taken to mean the ability to read aloud reasonably fluently and to read quietly with good understanding in a variety of printed materials. The importance of such remedial or basic literacy work is not in question here; indeed it is seen as a necessary precursor of silent reading that children should be able to read fluently in the 'aural' style. The point being made, however, is that it is necessary to go beyond this and develop some skill in using the different reading styles described in Chapter 5, and in using them appropriately in the light of the purpose for reading. The use of these styles in strategic approaches to reading tasks also needs attention.

As noted previously, many teachers will incidentally affect the development of silent reading in their pupils. For example, a teacher setting a reading task for homework may specify the purpose for reading in terms of what kind of information or understanding is required. If he fails to specify, then he encourages an unrealistic use of silent reading for he can imply that *all* the text must be read and known, as though understanding came from accretion of information rather than through a reorganization of the information which is taken in. If a test based on distinct factual items is given, then this misleading view of learning from silent reading is likely to be reinforced.

For a homework task it may often be appropriate to use receptive reading, but there are other styles of reading which might be positively developed in certain circumstances. For example, in revision for examinations it might be useful to encourage skimming and search reading rather than the plodding through text-books which often seems to take place. At other times scanning and search reading might be used for locating information, rather than having the teacher direct

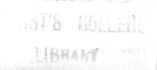

children to certain pages where relevant information appears. Especially, however, it is the excessive use of oral reading and the lack of use of uninterrupted silent reading which appears to militate against pupils developing the habit of using true silent reading, even where they might already possess some skill and may, indeed, already apply this skill in reading outside school.

The fact that teachers can incidentally affect silent reading development has been emphasized to stress the point that children are unlikely to develop effective silent reading behaviour if their perception of learning situations in school leads them to believe silent reading to be inappropriate. This is a major problem for any teacher who offers specialist courses in silent reading and who is concerned that what is learned shall transfer to tasks outside those in the specialist class. If the transfer does not take place, then it may well be that silent reading lessons will consist of no more than a few arid exercises done to please or appease the teacher.

However, despite the difficulties someone must take the lead, and the remainder of this section is concerned with a discussion of what specialist teachers of silent reading might teach. The methods to be used are dealt with separately since it is in many respects far more easy to devise methods for teaching than it is to clarify what precisely should be taught. The view of Wilson (1972) that much educational argument about method is really about what it is important to teach is a most useful one to bear in mind.

At some stage in secondary education attention must be paid to the use of sources of information such as libraries, reference books, dictionaries and other structured means of storing information for retrieval. This may be best done in the context of work in which children are involved elsewhere or it may be done using topics which are likely to be of interest and concern to them. The most important warning seems to be that simply telling children about such sources is unlikely to be of much help unless they have experience of using them. On the other hand, using them without either clear guidance or some very strong purpose (or preferably both) is likely to be fruitless and can also be frustrating (cf Neville and Pugh 1975c, 1977).

The use of sources of this kind is already given some attention in many secondary schools, although perhaps not always in an organized or effective way. However, it is the use of sources which are less structured which may need more attention, since there the extraction of information is a more complex task. Thus the styles of scanning and search reading need to be developed, as do the styles which less clearly involve location of information, such as receptive reading and skimming for the gist of a passage. The strategic use of these styles for learning and other purposes, and the use of previewing and skimming for deciding one's purpose and strategy also need attention.

What is difficult to decide is whether the use of these styles and strategies should be introduced at more or less the same time or whether there are certain styles and behaviours which are simpler than others, or on which others depend, and might therefore be introduced first. One reason why it is hard to be dogmatic about this is that the difficulty of a text, including such factors as the reader's knowledge of the topic and his interest in it as well as the linguistic and conceptual difficulty of the text, will have some effect upon the styles he can apply when reading it. However, it seems that the styles of scanning and search reading are less complex and might be introduced first, alongside the use of alphabeticized or otherwise clearly structured reference materials, whereas skimming and the strategic use of styles needs to be left until later. It may be that skimming needs to be preceded by practice leading to greater fluency in reading, as was felt to be the case in the course for students at Leeds (Chapter 5). However, with schoolchildren the time scale for developing fluency will almost certainly be considerably greater than it was in the case of the undergraduates, since with them there were grounds for thinking that one was drawing on a latent ability to increase rate in certain kinds of reading.

How might silent reading be taught in secondary schools?

If there are to be experiments in the teaching of silent reading in classes devoted specifically to it, then the teacher is likely to have to devise his own exercises. He might possibly consider incorporating some American materials of the kind listed by, for example, Miller (1972) but in general these will be inappropriate. Guidance given by American authors, such as Herber (1970) or Robinson (1975), might also be taken into account, although here again care would have to be taken in judging the appropriateness of their advice. The devising of silent reading tasks is therefore necessary and these must be incorporated into a framework so that the course has some structure. It will be borne in mind that we are not talking here of devising tests, but of tasks and exercises. The term test is deliberately avoided, in view of the difficulties in devising reliable and valid tests and care must be taken in interpreting results of any exercises which are devised, especially if they are marked by those who take them (cf Chapter 5).

For location of information, using scanning and search reading, it is relatively easy not only to set tasks but also to assess performance and to discuss the procedures which children have used. Receptive reading is more difficult to devise exercises for, since the measurement of comprehension and of time taken present problems, as does setting the purpose for reading. Receptive reading with schoolchildren should, perhaps, be less concerned with rate of reading and instead use longer passages of more realistic and relevant material than is common in the speed reading courses. Also, various kinds of questions might be used, such as free-response or forced-choice questions (with or without reference back to the text) and also summaries. The effect on learning of different types of questioning has been examined by Rothkopf and Kaplan (1972), among others. However, the important point to bear in mind here is that the type of question dictates the purpose for reading and that questions should not normally be asked which are inconsistent with the purpose set.

Variations in question density were referred to earlier, (Chapter 3). By reducing or increasing the number of questions some flexibility may develop as a result of relating rate of reading to purpose. Also, in developing skimming for surface information, it may be useful to begin by asking a small number of questions before the reading of the text in order to make the purpose in reading clear and to give an indication of the depth at which the text is to be read. These can be followed after reading by a far larger number of questions, many of which will be beyond the scope of the purpose originally set for reading and which, if answered correctly, will indicate that the reader has read too closely in relation to the purpose set.

Skimming in order to make decisions about whether to use a

text, and if so how to use it, can be tested by means of ability to answer questions or to justify the point of view taken. However, it may be possible to use this kind of activity in a more realistic task by having the reader act on his impressions of a text. Thus he might, for example, select from various sources the information needed for a report on a particular topic. The use of skimming in previewing for a text which must be studied in more detail can be described and practised, although how far the teacher would wish to enter into the field of note-taking and study technique is a question which is beyond our present scope. However, an important reservation might be made about the tendency of study skills courses to be unduly prescriptive and dogmatic, possibly as a result of their attempts to simplify and generalize. The emphasis, in this section as elsewhere, has been on giving experience of different styles of reading and in developing the ability in the reader to judge for himself their appropriateness in the light of what he is trying to achieve. Similarly it might be said of note-taking or other facets of learning that there are many different approaches, all or most of which are appropriate under certain conditions for effective study. It is not so much a question of having *the* right technique or method as of knowing which of many approaches is appropriate for what one is trying to achieve in a particular task.

Conclusion and summary

The questions raised in this chapter are not easy to resolve because of lack of precedent for the teaching of silent reading in British schools. It has been argued that the teaching must be the responsibility of someone, and that the use of special classes or courses may well be necessary, even though there are dangers in that transfer to other reading tasks might not take place. On the other hand, it has been suggested that the transfer depends upon schools themselves making more use of silent reading. This vicious circle seems unlikely to be broken unless some take the lead and draw attention to the importance of silent reading by teaching it.

What precisely is to be taught clearly requires much more thought, as do the methods to be used in the teaching. The suggestions made here, based largely on experience with undergraduates and which can be amplified by reference to earlier chapters in this book, do not provide a ready-made course for schools. They are of necessity tentative since, until experience in the teaching of silent reading in schools accrues, it will be necessary to borrow ideas judiciously from areas where the teaching of silent reading has been somewhat better established.

7

Comprehension, Readability and Reading Interests

Comprehension, readability and reading interests have usually been studied as if they were distinct areas and each has accrued its own considerable literature. In fact the three areas are more closely related to each other than the literature might suggest, for in all three the main concern is to assess how the text affects the reader. Thus it is possible for studies in these areas to cast light on the reader's interaction with a text and hence increase understanding of what happens during reading.

The concerns of those working in these areas have normally been more practical, however. Comprehension as investigated and defined for purposes of constructing comprehension tests has tended to refer to what has been gained from reading a text, normally as assessed by responses to questions given after reading. Thus the ongoing process of comprehending texts, and questions of comprehensibility in texts have received less attention from those interested in reading comprehension. Readability research is concerned with comprehensibility to some extent, in that it attempts to discover ways of predicting how easy or difficult it is likely to be for a reader or group of readers to read a text. Reading interests have usually been studied by asking children or adults what they have enjoyed reading although some attempts have been made to predict reading interests by means of general interest inventories or attitude scales.

In view of the extent of what has been written on comprehension, readability and reading interests, it is only possible here to provide an introduction to the topics and the work which has been done on them, and to point out links between the three areas.

Comprehension

Comprehension is, of course, necessary and essential for effective silent reading. Yet, as Golinkoff (1976) remarks, it is an area which, until recently, was somewhat neglected even though eminent earlier researchers into silent reading, such as Buswell (1920) and Anderson (1937), certainly regarded reading as a process involving extraction of meaning. Nevertheless, as Chapter 8 suggests, most writers of this earlier period did not investigate comprehension very fully. In particular, they tended not to examine very closely the phenomenon of reading in various ways to achieve various purposes. Hence they were often content to accept some rather general measure of comprehension.

Much of the more recent literature on comprehension similarly ignores purpose and tends to seek for a definition of comprehension in terms of skilled behaviour which accompanies (or is integrated into) reading. Global definitions of comprehension are as dangerous, it might well be argued, as are global definitions of reading. Awareness of this by some researchers has led to the major debate over comprehension, between those who hold that comprehension is a unitary process or skill and, more common among those concerned with the teaching of reading, that it comprises various sub-skills.

It may be noted at this stage, however, that there is a school of thought which holds that comprehension is not an accurate or proper term. Quiller-Couch (1920, Ch. 2) argued that the term apprehension is more appropriate, especially when reading literary material, for to comprehend rather than apprehend implies an arrogance on the part of the reader. Another literary critic and philosopher, I. A. Richards (1924, p. 132) wrote of those 'permanent modifications in the structure of the mind which works of art can produce'. These permanent modifications are beyond the range of most researchers who have been concerned with measuring reading comprehension, possibly because such effects do not lend themselves to observation or measurement, and it is measurement of reading comprehension which has been the main concern of most who have contributed to the literature.

However, it is clearly necessary in order to measure a quality to have it (at least operationally) defined. We are now, therefore, concerned with attempts to define comprehension and especially with the debate as to whether comprehension consists of sub-skills or is a unitary skill. The means available for measuring reading comprehension are examined (albeit briefly) in the next chapter, since they are more conveniently considered alongside tests of reading, of which they normally form part.

It must be noted before considering theories of comprehension that in British and American schools comprehension tends to be looked at in slightly different ways. In Britain, the practice in schools has usually been to measure comprehension by means of free-response answers to a passage which is still available to the reader. More recently, multiple-choice questions have become more common, mainly perhaps for ease and reliability of marking. The practice in the United States has normally been to use multiple-choice questions after the text has been removed. In other words recall has been involved as well as understanding. This difference has been found by P. E. Vernon (1962) to influence test taking when groups of both nationalities were compared on various types of comprehension test. From our present point of view, it should urge caution among British readers in interpreting findings or theories based on American research.

Theories of comprehension

In a most thorough review of psychometric research on comprehension in reading Davis (1972) distinguishes between three approaches to the analysis of comprehension in reading. These approaches are: broad subjective analyses, which Davis notes are sometimes called 'arm-chair' analyses; subjective analyses based on specific studies; and multivariate analyses (using specialized statistical procedures such as regression analysis and factor analysis).

The subjective 'arm-chair' analyses include those of Bloom *et al.* (1956) which is well known from the *Taxonomy of Educational Objectives* and Barrett (given in Clymer, 1968) which has gained considerable currency in this country through its adoption in the Open University's course in Reading Development (Course no. PE261). Both Barrett and Bloom, along with many other writers, give a list of behaviours in reading comprehension which appear to overlap to some extent. The more complex behaviours seem to include the simpler ones almost as though a hierarchy of behaviours might exist. Thus Bloom gives remembering, reasoning, problem solving, concept formation, and creative thinking; Barrett suggests as main headings literal comprehension, reorganization, inferential comprehension, evaluation, and appreciation. Clymer (1968), who reports Barrett's taxonomy fully, notes that it draws heavily on Bloom, among others. However, this would necessarily be so, for subjective analyses will tend to be influenced by each other. Indeed, the general drift of the lists and taxonomies of many later writers, can be seen in the eight purposes for reading given by Gray (1919). These range from reading to give a coherent reproduction to reading to determine the validity of statements, and are similar in their pattern and range to the development in Barrett's taxonomy from literal comprehension to evaluation.

While noting that the 'arm-chair' analysts were aware of the empirical work done in testing reading comprehension, Davis nevertheless stresses that broadly based subjective analyses are mainly useful for guiding those who construct measuring instruments which, he says, will be validated 'against reality'. The problem in this area is, of course, in deciding what constitutes the reality against which measures of comprehension can be validated. Without taking too far the socially constructed theory of reality proposed by Berger and Luckman (1966), it is nevertheless clear that comprehension itself (i.e. 'real' as opposed to measured comprehension) is a construct and not something which has any existence in itself. All the same it might be as well to heed the warning given by Davis against the common practice of using these unvalidated analyses as the basis for learning exercises, if only because the analyses are not always in operationalizable form.

During the last sixty years a considerable number of studies have been carried out both in attempts to substantiate the types of sub-skills of comprehension which researchers considered might exist, and by analysing the responses of children or adults to determine the areas in which they appeared to comprehend poorly and thus to derive a list of skills for teaching comprehension. The refinements of statistical procedures (and presumably the availability of calculating machines and later computers) permitted the use of very much larger samples and a greater number of variables in attempts to predict what factors related closely to reading comprehension, as well as providing a means of discovering what (if any) were the separate sub-skills or types of comprehension. The main researches in this field were by Holmes (1954), Singer (1965), Holmes and Singer (1966) and Davis himself (1944, 1968).

Davis concludes from his review that there are several factors which can be identified for purposes of teaching and testing and which must be taken into account in considering the nature of comprehension. Few of the studies he reviews appear to disagree, except on the hierarchical view of comprehension referred to above, which Davis considers not inconsistent with his findings. Unfortunately, the situation is not so clearcut as this for both Spearritt (1972) and R. L. Thorndike (1973), to whose work Spearritt had access, have questioned Davis's position and procedure and have reworked his data. Thorndike found that of the many sub-skills postulated only word knowledge (vocabulary) stands out clearly as a factor for predicting reading comprehension with 12th grade students (i.e. those aged about 18 years). Using rather more refined procedures Spearritt is led to conclude that what is measured in tests of reading comprehension, as distinct from word knowledge tests, is something which might be labelled 'reasoning in reading'.

Recent work in Britain by Lunzer, Waite and Dolan (1977) concludes even more strongly that sub-skills in comprehension do not exist. Indeed, they argue that using the term 'skill' for comprehension is misleading since comprehension does not serve as a label or description for anything which the reader actually does. Rather than describing an event in time, they state, it characterizes an achievement. Successful comprehension in realistic reading (as opposed to a test) comes, according to this view, from appropriate application of a number of operations such as, for example, decoding, judging, questioning and so forth.

It was noted earlier in this chapter that most work in the field of reading comprehension has been undertaken by people with the practical concerns of teaching and testing in mind. It would appear, however, from the criticisms made of the sub-skill view that many definitions of comprehension have in fact been somewhat misleading for teachers and researchers. Farr (1969) gives support to this view, when he argues that a great many of the so-called separate reading skills which are tested are very highly interdependent.

Teaching reading comprehension

If this is so, important questions arise about the teaching of comprehension. For example, if comprehension is a unitary factor, how can it be developed if its elements cannot be identified? Must one rely merely on practice and maturation, or can help be given? The answers are by no means clear, especially when the questions are put in this way. Perhaps, if the view of Lunzer, Waite and Dolan is correct, there may be value in questioning which draws attention to those operations which are necessary for comprehension to occur, although these researchers might reject this view as tending to come too close to applications (with which they may not be in sympathy) of taxonomies such as those of Barratt and Bloom.

The solution that has been argued in this book is in accord with the view that comprehension is best regarded as a state of achievement, rather than as an activity or a skill which is applied to texts. By stressing the different strategies and styles of reading which are appropriate for achieving various goals, one breaks away from the apparent *impasse* into which many of the discussions of comprehension lead. The question of deciding between the unitary skill and the sub-skill theories appears less important than the devising of means of assessing how well particular purposes are achieved and, of course, of how best to define those purposes.

Lunzer, Waite and Dolan consider that many difficulties in the field of comprehension are due to the tests and the position in which they place the reader. One might note especially that many tests of comprehension are so constructed that the reader only realizes the purpose for reading when he sees the questions. Where, as in American practice, the text is removed so that he must answer from recall, he is unable to make use of the purpose which the questions define for him as an aid in reading the text. Thus the validity of many approaches to measurement of reading comprehension is suspect, and the teaching of sub-skills whose existence is doubtful seems not only questionable but, in silent reading at least, may betray lack of awareness of what is involved in reading in more normal stiuations than the classroom or when taking a test.

Such a condemnation may well be too strong, and it certainly should not lead one to disregard or dismiss the literature on reading comprehension. Nevertheless, it has been a consistent theme in this book that transfer of learning from reading courses appears unlikely where operational considerations have led to a narrow definition of reading being adopted. Comprehension, which is intimately related to silent reading, seems to have suffered somewhat similarly.

Readability

Readability is taken here to refer to the linguistic and conceptual difficulty of texts, as opposed to their legibility. Studies of legibility factors such as typography and design have been reviewed by several writers, notably Burt (1959), Tinker (1965), Spencer (1969), and Watts and Nisbet (1974). Unfortunately, even in this field the findings often appear to be inconclusive owing to the difficulties of controlling the many variables which operate. In the field of readability, however, most writers have felt less unsure about the validity of the findings, although there are some doubts about the reliability of measures used and some important questions about how these measures are validated.

The concern with predicting how difficult or easy a child or children will find a text goes back, no doubt, more than a century to the first large-scale production of series of reading books. However, it was not until the 1920s that any significant attempt was made to put the assessment and prediction of difficulty on an objective basis. Initially the method favoured was the use of word lists and of these the best known perhaps are those of Thorndike (1932) and West (1927). Word frequency methods are still in use both in research by, for example, Culhane (1976) who compared Russian and English texts, but more obviously perhaps as a basis for reading schemes. Indeed, the best known word list in this country is almost certainly that of McNally and Murray (1962) on which the Ladybird Key Words reading scheme is based.

Since about 1940, there has been a movement away from word

lists towards the use of formulae which take into account syntactic as well as (or instead of) semantic features of a text. Full details of many of the formulae are available in Klare (1963 and 1974), and Gilliland (1972). Also Harrison (1977) provides a useful introduction. All that will be offered here, therefore, is a description of the basic features of the formulae and some assessment of their validity and usefulness.

In considering what makes for ease or difficulty, there are clearly a very large number of factors which could be taken into account. These include such matters as whether the reader is already interested in what a book is about, whether the book is written in such a way that it is likely to create interest, whether there are conceptual problems and/or problems in expression, and so on. Most formulae for predicting reading ease or difficulty have taken account of only a small number of these factors. In the main they have considered the frequency with which a word occurs in the language and the complexity of the sentence. A further step is to use letter or syllable counts instead of word counts, on the grounds that the more common words tend to be the shorter words. Similarly, sentence length rather than structure is normally what is assessed, on the grounds that shorter sentences tend to be less complex than longer ones. This reduction in the number of factors measured can be criticized, and examples of short difficult sentences are not hard to find. Descartes' 'I think, therefore I am' or St John's 'In the beginning was the Word' are two which come to mind where the simplicity of sentence structure and the familiarity of the words conceal considerable philosophical difficulty. Nevertheless, there is evidence (cited by Klare, 1968) of high negative correlation between length of words and their frequency of occurence in English prose. The relationship between sentence length and complexity of sentence structure appears to be less well established, perhaps because it has seemed too obvious to be worth establishing or possibly because of the difficulty of agreeing means of analysing sentences.

Readability formulae

A simple readability formula which may be given as an example is the Fog Index (Gunning, 1952). For this, one takes three samples of 100 words from a text and in each sample counts the number of sentences and the number of words of three or more syllables (excluding obvious compounds). The average sentence length can then be calculated and to this is added the number of 'hard' words (i.e. words of three or more syllables). Multiplying this sum by 0.4 gives a quotient which is claimed to be close to the American grade level for which the text is suitable.

Other formulae work on basically similar principles, although some (notably Flesch, 1948) introduce a measure of human interest by counting the personal words. Other variations include the retention of word lists (instead of calculating word length) and this is possible where formulae have been designed or revised for ease of computing. Indeed the use of computers for obtaining readability measures has not only served to make them more readily available for use by, for example, publishers and industrial companies with technical writing departments, but has also permitted a more ready comparison between the different formulae. This in turn has provided some information relevant to considering their validity.

As might be expected, since the formulae work on similar principles, results from application of several formulae to the same text reveal high intercorrelations (Harrison, 1977). Klare (1974) also reports some high correlations between formulae in cross validation studies. What is a little more disturbing is that, according to Klare and Macdonald-Ross (1976), the standard errors of published formulae range from 0.38 to 2.37 grades at least. If a formula has a standard error of exactly one year or one grade level, this means that in approximately one case in three it will give a figure which is more than one year too high or too low. In fact Harrison (1977) considers that the standard error for most formulae is between 0.7 and 0.85 grades, which is not much below the example of one school year given above and which clearly suggests that care should be taken in considering the results obtained using these formulae. Indeed, even greater caution must be urged in the light of the fact that the standard errors quoted often appear to be óbtained by applying formulae to certain graded test passages (notably the *Standard Test Lessons in Reading*, McCall and Crabbs, 1925). Thus, in general it is not the internal consistency on normal prose which has been taken into account. In some recently published work at the Open

University, Stokes (1978) has addressed himself to this problem and has found considerable variations between formulae and within formulae, when a number of measures of readability were taken on a sample from each page of several school textbooks.

Clearly the reliability of readability formulae is open to question and it would assist if full validation data were given, as for performance tests, in reporting formulae. In particular, information is needed about how the validation is done, that is whether it is by reference to graded reading schemes, by comparing findings with teachers' judgements, by using passages as for comprehension tests and seeing how well children perform, or by using cloze procedure versions of the text with children and assessing their performance. Finally, clarification is needed as to what the grade level or quotient produced by a formula is thought to predict about readers' possible ability to cope with a text. It seems to be sometimes thought that a formula really predicts readability (as opposed to unintelligibility). If so, then a result which predicted a text to be readable for say the average 9-year-old would suggest that it would be unreadable for the half of the children of nine years old who are below average.

The problems encountered in attempting to validate formulae are similar to those encountered by legibility researchers. They are caused by the difficulty of measuring reading behaviour and what is gained from reading. It is in this connection that the cloze procedure became popular as a testing device, since the comprehension questions are not separate from the text but are, as it were, an integral part of it. Cloze procedure has also been used as a part of readability formulae as Klare (1974) points out. It can also, like all other criteria for validating readability formulae, be used instead of them. Perhaps the main advocate of using cloze procedure as a readability measure is Bormuth (1968) who has elsewhere (Bormuth, 1973) strongly argued the advantages of cloze procedure in testing reading performance.

Usefulness and limitations of readability measures

A number of uses have been suggested for readability measures. Gunning (1952) saw readability formulae as of use to writers, although Klare has consistently emphasized the dangers of attempting to write to a formula. Originally, however, the formulae and the word-lists were intended as an aid in the selection of materials, especially texts for school books and for books for foreign-speaking learners of English. It is this use which is still most commonly advocated, but it must be questioned whether the formulae are very suitable for choosing texts for silent reading exercises of the type referred to in earlier chapters.

In attempting to choose passages for students on the reading courses at the University of Leeds, readability formulae were not found to be a useful guide. This was often because factors beyond the sentence level were important for tasks such as scanning and search reading where the typographical presentation of the material and its structural organization were of importance. Similarly, with passages for receptive reading at speed there appeared to be difficulties. Pritchatt (1971), also at the University of Leeds, had stressed the need for such passages to be tested under the conditions in which they were to be used. The importance of the conditions is taken further by Hittleman (1973) who argues that readability is not an entity inherent in a passage, but is related rather 'to a "moment" at which the reader's emotional, cognitive and linguistic backgrounds interact with each other, with the topic, with the proposed purpose for doing the reading, and with the author's choice of semantic and syntactic structure' (p. 778).

The parallel between Hittleman's view of readability as a moment and of the view of comprehension as achievement which Lunzer, Waite and Dolan (1977) put forward is an interesting one. Hittleman appears to be talking about readability in terms similar to those used by Lunzer *et al.* to refer to comprehension. In doing so he emphasizes the difficulty of observing that process and, by stressing the large number of inaccessible factors, appears to discourage measurement. Whatever the merits of this criticism of readability, there does nevertheless appear to be a place for some further work in the field, and especially in providing descriptions of texts. The limitation of the readability formulae from the point of view of selecting texts for silent reading is that they do not provide enough information to help in choosing texts for reading for different purposes. Unfortunately, the science of linguistics has not been very helpful in providing descriptions beyond the level of the sentence or perhaps the paragraph, although interest in this area has increased recently. Indeed

Halliday and Hasan (1976) propose a means of describing virtually any text, but so far their approach does not appear very helpful for the purposes mentioned here.

Reading interests

Interest in reading is fairly generally acknowledged to be of importance to reading development. As already noted, some readability formulae take interest into account, albeit at the level of 'human interest' in a text. A number of writers have argued or shown that readability and interest are connected in another way, in that more difficult texts appear to be less interesting for children. Thus for example, Allard (1946, cited Klare 1963) used seven hundred poems with a sample of 50,000 elementary schoolchildren and found a negative correlation between preference and vocabulary difficulty.

Another aspect of difficulty is not so much due to linguistic as to cultural factors. A number of writers, among them Alderson (1968), Yarlott and Harpin (1971) and Pugh (1969, 1971) have investigated the leisure reading of children and related this to the kind of material read in school. Pugh suggested that the distaste for schoolbooks found among some children who read a great deal on their own may well create, as well as mirror, a general distaste for school. Certainly, far too little attention appears to have been paid to the study by teachers of the reading materials which children enjoy and one may surmise that a cultural gap exists. This has, oddly enough, not been helped by the few writers of distinction such as Orwell (1940) and Hoggart (1957) who have made a study of popular reading materials, since they tend to condemn contemporary popular material while elevating the popular ephemeral literature of the past.

Some evidence that children have difficulty in understanding literary texts at the kind of level which is expected is given in Barnes *et al.* (1971) where children were tape-recorded as they discussed a novel, *Day of the Triffids* (Wyndham 1951). Much of the time of these fifteen-year-old pupils appears to have been spent in sorting out the plot. Possibly, however, this is partly due to the fact that books were being read by a group, rather than selected individually. An answer was suggested by Fader (1966) in the United States to the lack of interest in reading, due perhaps to both linguistic and cultural problems, among boys in a reformatory school. This involved promoting the ownership of books as well as having the teachers encourage free choice and express interest in what was read.

Most studies of reading interests have, however, been of the survey research type. That is to say that the emphasis has been on collecting data about reading interests and habits, rather than addressing any particular problem relating to reading interests. One of the most extensive pieces of research in this field was sponsored by the Schools Council and carried out at Sheffield University into the reading habits of children between ten and fifteen years old (Whitehead, Capey and Maddren, 1975); the earliest British study appears to be that of Jenkinson (1940). A useful review of a number of studies is offered by D'Arcy (1973) and a slightly more up-to-date one is in Hayes (1975). What appears to emerge is that there is a considerable influence of fashion especially in children's stated book reading preferences and that voluntary reading choices are also affected by factors such as sex, age, type of education and environment. However, interesting as much of this information is, it does not immediately suggest any course of action or indeed provide answers to the problem of lack of interest.

Another criticism of this kind of research is that questions such as 'Who is your favourite author?' or 'How many books have you read in the last month?' are not likely to obtain very reliable answers. Even if the respondent attempts to be honest, it is likely that inability to remember precisely, or a desire to provide some kind of acceptable answer, will result in some risk of the questions obtaining false responses. Thus the apparently consistent popularity of Enid Blyton's books (both in Britain and in Austria—see Binder, 1976) may be partly due to the fact that the author's name is well known to children, and only to some extent evidence of what certain commentators regard as children's poor taste.

Attempts to determine taste in literary texts have, of course, long formed an essential part of the teaching of English. More recently there has been a great increase in concern among adults about children's literature, i.e. books specifically written for children. However, one should beware of assuming that this trend represents an awareness of the likes and needs of children.

The gulf between the juries for children's literature prizes and the children may well be considerable (*see* Pugh, 1973 for some evidence on this) as, it has been suggested, is the gulf which sometimes exists between what teachers consider suitable for children and what children themselves choose to read.

One can criticize the study of reading interests for concentrating too much upon simply discovering what has been read. However, Yarlott and Harpin (1971) suggest that teachers for their part have been too concerned with a 'tendency to prescribe what "ought" to be read without any regard to how the prescription relates to the pupil's immediate interests and concerns and to his own reading preferences' (p. 96). One way out of this dilemma is suggested by an approach developed by media researchers in reaction to the head-counting which has sometimes typified survey research methods but which has not been found fruitful in attempts to discover whether films or television harm children.

The 'uses and gratifications' approach (*see* e.g. McQuail, 1969; IPC 1975) concentrates less upon what media do to people than with what people do with what the media present. This functional approach has been used in this country in investigating children's use of television by, for example, Noble (1975). Noble discerned varied patterns of viewing behaviour from subject to subject and he considered some of the patterns related to personality. Brown, Cramond and Wilde (1973) examined the incidence of use made by schoolchildren of various media (including printed media) in relation to the purposes for which they used them. They found certain conditions under which certain media were frequently used, but more interesting, perhaps, was the wide range of permutations of media and uses among their sample of 800 children.

Little work has been done in the field of attitudes and reading, as a useful review by Alexander and Filler (1977) indicates. There appear to be problems in distinguishing what aspects of reading should be considered in relation to attitudes, and the assessment of personality characteristics also presents considerable difficulties (*see* Vernon, 1964). However, it seems that it is in this area of assessing the deeper effects of reading on individuals that future work in reading interests must lie, if only because the survey research approach has failed to provide very useful information.

Conclusion and summary

This chapter has been concerned with three related areas of study which have bearing not so much on the physical act of reading as on the effect of reading upon the reader. As far as possible, detailed questions relating to the measurement of comprehension, readability and reading interests have been avoided yet it has nevertheless been necessary to refer several times to the problems of measurement which pose so much difficulty in research into reading.

Some relatively unusual suggestions have been made here about the inter-relatedness of the three areas. Attention has also been drawn to the limitations of measures of comprehension and the theories relating to them; the validity of readability measures has been queried and the need for better descriptions of texts emphasized. It has been argued, with regard to reading interest, that we need to consider not only the child consumer view of what he is offered to read, but to go further and attempt to find patterns and reasons in individual children's preferences. These suggestions are, of course, mainly for further research but the issues are ones with which the teacher of silent reading needs to be familiar especially in devising exercises, assessing tests and interpreting their results, choosing texts and in promoting interest in reading.

8

The Study and Measurement of Silent Reading Performance

This chapter considers experimental methods for observing, recording and assessing silent reading behaviour, and also looks at testing techniques. The testing of silent reading is not merely of interest to researchers or to those concerned with diagnosis and remediation of special problems in reading. It is also of great concern to teachers of reading since, as has already been seen, the definitions of behaviours such as comprehension often derive from test constructors. Similarly, as was noted in discussing speed reading courses, what is tested has a considerable influence on what is taught. Thus the validity of reading tests must be of concern to teachers attempting to teach silent reading.

At the practical level of devising exercises for silent reading, the teacher can also benefit from a knowledge of test construction, and of the ideas employed in testing silent reading. Study of the visual behaviour used during silent reading might also suggest approaches to devising exercises, although research into visual behaviour perhaps serves more to emphasize the elusive nature of silent reading.

*Eye-movement research**

As noted in earlier chapters, the study of visual behaviour has been of considerable interest to psychologists during much of this century. It is true that, as Gibson and Levin (1975) point out, the main interest of reading researchers has been in curriculum issues from about 1920 until very recently. Nevertheless, a considerable amount of experience and expertise in methodology for studying eye-movements during reading has accrued. However, because of the curriculum concerns of those concerned with teaching

*Some of the information in this and the following section is from Pugh (1977b).

reading, the research has not influenced practice greatly. Nor was it likely to do so because it was often not directly concerned with practice.

The visual activity in reading is, of course, no more than the visible tip of far less accessible behaviour, and the view that reading performance can be radically improved by changes in visual techniques is now largely discredited (Tinker, 1965). Nevertheless, methods used in studying visual behaviour can provide information for individual diagnosis as well as producing evidence which may lead to a better understanding of the processes and activities involved in silent reading.

The many studies in the field of eye-movement research have been reviewed by a number of writers, most of whom give fairly detailed attention to the methodology. Apart from the early review of Huey (1908), there are others by M. D. Vernon (1931), Carmichael and Dearborn (1948) and Tinker (1965) which are particularly concerned with the study of eye-movements in reading. A more recent work by Yarbus (1967) is also useful, although not mainly concerned with reading.

Ditchburn (1973), who specifically excludes reading, nevertheless gives a useful indication of approaches to studying eye-movements. According to Ditchburn (1973, p. 37ff) there are four main methods commonly used for studying large eye-movements. Two of them, the corneal reflection method and the scleral observation method, require the subject's head to be fixed, as did most of the methods used in earlier studies of reading running text (as opposed to isolated words, letters or other symbols). Of the other methods, the after-image method requires only simple apparatus, but has the disadvantage for the study of reading that a relatively bright light must be shone into the eyes, whereas the corneo-retinal potential method requires electrodes to be attached to the subject. Other methods, considered by most researchers to be more suitable for the study of smaller eye-movements, require some attachment to the subject's eye. There appears to be justification for the remark of Yarbus (1967, p. 58) that 'none of the methods which have proved successful can be regarded as universal and perfect'. Indeed, all appear to have fairly serious limitations for the study of silent reading, although they clearly have considerable uses in other areas of research.

The main limitations of the methods are not related so much to accuracy, which is the main concern of those interested in eye-movements *per se*, but rather to the validity of the experimental situation and of the tasks suited to it. Often, as indicated, the subject must keep his head still and be surrounded by apparatus. Special lighting may be needed and the text must often be fixed in one position. In much of the early work in reading, the subject was obliged to read line by line, since if he failed to do so the record became difficult to interpret. Some of these difficulties have been partly overcome and some relatively portable apparatus is now commercially available. A useful review is given by Young and Sheena (1975) who (pp. 326–327) provide a tabulated comparison of techniques for eye-movement measurement. One recent approach which they consider promising in many respects, utilizes differential measurements of corneal reflection and reflection from the pupil centre. Illumination is often infra-red, the subject has more freedom of head movement than is normal and recording is by television camera. A fuller description of such a method is given by Monty (1975) but it will be noted that the text or stimulus is presented by back-projection. Nevertheless, this approach may well be useful for studying silent reading especially where the relative lack of accuracy, precision and speed which Young and Sheena note is less important.

Three recent methods for studying adult silent reading

Many of the writers who have studied eye-movements have, of course, been aware of the limitations already referred to, and there have been some attempts in the past to study adult silent reading under more normal and less restricted conditions, as Carmichael and Dearborn (1948) in particular indicate. During the past few years, a few British researchers have also been concerned with reading under relatively normal conditions and most of this section is devoted to a review of methods used in three of these studies. Two of these were related to attempts to help undergraduates to read more efficiently, and one was in the field of studying textual design.

In the latter area, Whalley developed a method for examining the effect on reading behaviour of the position of diagrams in a text. His method (Whalley and Fleming, 1975) entails the subject reading with a hand-guided torch which illuminates the area which the reader wishes to see clearly. The surroundings are darkened so that the text is not clearly visible without using the torch. The torch beam is set in such a way that three lines of one column are illuminated but there is a facility whereby the subject can increase this area so that scanning is not unduly constrained. A later development was to attach the torch by a rod to a joy-stick control assembly. The movement can then be translated into electrical impulses which may be recorded onto magnetic tape or fed directly into a computer for on-line analysis. Various types of graphical output of the data have been used. These can show either point-by-point movement over the page, or a record of overall movement over the page and the cumulative time spent.

The use of a light is clearly somewhat unnatural for the reader, and the recording of page turns requires another method (in this case by sensors within the reading table). Nevertheless, the restrictions on the subject are less than in most of the eye-movement recording methods. Larger amounts of text can be used and, although accuracy is reduced, the task itself is reasonably close to a real reading task. Whalley has also paid particular attention to ease and accuracy of analysis. More recently, with a view to application to the Open University, he has been examining methods which could be used as part of a home kit, so that students could be studied in their usual surroundings. One approach he has suggested is a means of recording page turns in long texts, with a timing facility (Whalley, 1976). As in the earlier experiment with the torch method, the reader's purpose, and to some extent his style of reading, can be set by taking a realistic task. However, the problem of assessing what the subject achieves from the task, as opposed to how he carries out the task, has still to be overcome.

Some work carried out over a number of years in the Centre for Human Learning at Brunel University has paid attention both to recording behaviour and assessing performance (Thomas and Harri-Augstein, 1976; Thomas, Augstein and Farnes, 1975). The Reading Recorder developed at Brunel utilizes text printed on continuous stationery and visible to the reader a segment at a time. It incorporates a recording device showing the reader's position in the text against time. A later addition was a note pad on a sensitized switch which permitted recording not only of the reading behaviour, but also of where the subject took notes.

Although the text is not in book form, and the form it is in may serve to encourage a sequential approach to reading, nevertheless the reader is in a more normal situation than with the eye-movement recording experiments.

The apparatus appears mainly to have been used for action research work, where the aim has been to give students some information on how they approached a text, in part by comparing their reading records with those of other students. The understanding of a text has been tested by means of questions asked after the text and by means of summaries. Generally it has been found that those who do well on summaries also do well on the questions, but that the reverse is not true. The use of flow charts to indicate the reader's structuring of the text has been extensively used and appears to permit of comparisons, while also allowing different levels or types of reading of the same text according to the depth and detail required.

An adaptation of the principles of the recorder to a pencil and paper technique has been made and has been used in one of the Open University's courses (Thomas and Augstein, 1973). However, this adaptation of the method is less objective and accurate than the recorder itself, for it relies on an observer whose presence may also be somewhat distracting to the reader.

A different approach was devised by the writer in studies related to the course at the University of Leeds which was intended to help students improve their efficiency in reading. (*See* Chapter 5.) Apparatus was built in order to study the different styles used by readers in attempting to locate information within books. This type of task, where the questions are given in advance, ensures that the subjects are explicitly given similar purposes for reading. Also their achievement can be checked in terms of what they were meant to be doing.

The apparatus, suggested by a method used by Karslake (1940), consists of a video-camera, recorder and monitor, together with a specially made reading stand. The stand, which is placed on a table, is made of wood and Pilkington Solarshield 15/23 glass. The glass, which forms the upper part of the stand has high reflective qualities. By lighting the under part of the glass it is possible to obtain a high quality reflected image of the subject's head while, owing to the lighting and angle, the glass in the stand does not appear to him to be a mirror. The apparatus has been used with undergraduates (Pugh, 1974), sixth formers (Pugh, 1976) and middle schoolchildren (Neville and Pugh, 1975c and 1977). Its major disadvantage is that although it provides a method of recording, it does not record data in a form ready for analysis. However, its main advantage is that the reading can be done under more normal conditions than with most other methods.

Of the methods and approaches available for observing and recording silent reading behaviour, all seem to have certain limitations. Especially insofar as the methods appear to impose or encourage certain styles of reading, findings from them should be interpreted with caution. In order to describe fully the range of activities undertaken by the skilled silent reader it may be necessary to use a range of methods, even though this is costly and inconvenient. However accurate the record of visual behaviour, problems still remain in assessing what a reader has gained from a text. At present one may set the reader a purpose and see whether or how well he achieves it, or rely on responses to questions asked after the reading, or interpret notes made during the reading. Whatever the approach, the precision with which it is possible to record visual behaviour is not possible here, and it must be noted, of course, that the kind of task given has itself some effect upon the visual behaviour. Nevertheless, the study of visual behaviour by means of recording silent reading performance has many applications, not only at the level of improving understanding and developing theory. It could, for example, lead to the student or pupil receiving fairly accurate feedback on his reading performance.

Testing silent reading

Much of the research into reading behaviour has been concerned less with giving feedback to students than with attempting to record more accurately than is possible in tests the activity of silent reading. In a sense, therefore, the aim has been to validate tests, or provide information against which they could be validated. Tests of silent reading are unlike those of oral reading, in that it is normally necessary with silent reading tests to infer the process from the product, for example to determine whether someone has read a passage thoroughly (which is a process) from his ability to answer questions (which is a product, albeit a product contaminated by other factors). In the testing of oral reading, the physical activity of reading is itself scrutinized and so the physical, though not the mental, activity is observed and can be recorded by the tester. In testing silent reading more complex, and sometimes very ingenious, methods have been necessary.

It would be wrong to give the impression that a great many tests of silent reading are available. In this country only one test is at present in print for use with university and college students, and there are relatively few for secondary schoolchildren. Pumfrey (1976) provided a useful review of reading tests available in Britain and in his section on attainment and diagnostic tests lists forty tests of British origin. Of these only eleven have norms for reading ages as high as 16 years and some of the eleven are out of print or are not tests of silent reading at all. Thus it appears that very few British tests of silent reading are in fact available.

The situation in the United States is a little different, since many tests of various aspects of reading are available. Indeed, there are so many as to warrant a separate publication devoted solely to reading tests (Buros, 1968) taken from *The Mental Measurements Handbook*, which is the standard American work for lists and reviews of most psychometric instruments. Also the range of different types of tests of silent reading is greater in the United States than in Britain, although none of this should be taken to suggest that the ratio of oral reading tests to silent reading tests differs much between these two countries.

Principles used in testing silent reading

There are several basic principles, and many permutations of these principles, employed in testing silent reading. Rather than list the tests separately, the approach taken here is to look at the basic principles and to refer to the most well-known tests for exemplification.

Perhaps the most obvious way to test silent reading is to give a passage for reading and then to ask some questions on the passage. Black's *Comprehension Test for College of Education Students* (Black, 1954) adopts this approach and uses seven passages, each of which is followed by a number of questions, mainly of the multiple-choice type. *The Manchester Reading Comprehension Test (Senior) I* (Wiseman and Wrigley, 1959) was similar in kind (although Pumfrey notes that it is now out of print), and the same principles are found in Haward's *Reading Comprehension Test for Personnel Selection* (Haward, 1965) and certain of the tests in batteries by Watts (1944), Schonell and Schonell (1962) and Bate (1965). The devising of tests consisting of passages followed by questions was undertaken by Lunzer, Waite and Dolan (1977) who were referred to in the discussion of comprehension in Chapter 7.

Similar principles are followed by Neale (1958) except that her test passages can be used for oral reading or silent reading and may also be used to assess speed. In general, however, the British tests of this kind are untimed, in that no attempt is made to discover rate of reading or time spent on answering questions, provided of course that the test is completed within the time allowed. There are exceptions, for Bate (1965) attempted to measure speed or rate by inserting questions into his texts and taking account of the last question which the child answered. A similar approach is used in the *Edinburgh Reading Tests, Stage 2* (Hutchings and Hutchings, 1972).

American testers have been much more concerned with rate of reading, and one approach often favoured, if much criticized, has been to discover how many words a student can read in one minute. Thus the relatively recent revision (Nelson, Denny and Brown, 1960) of a test originally published in 1924 provides parallel forms for grades 9 to 16+ (i.e. from age 14 upwards) to measure a number of aspects of reading. In the section where rate is measured the student stops reading after one minute, and subsequently goes on to complete the passage and answer questions. Buros (1968) lists a number of other tests which are similar to the Nelson-Denny in that they are old battery tests for a wide age range. Some, such as the Iowa Silent Reading Test (Greene, Jorgensen and Kelley, 1942) measured rate on a one-minute sample, although this has disappeared from the latest version of this test where there is now 'a five-minute time limit for six passages containing forty embedded multiple-choice selections for modified cloze tests of comprehension'. (Ransom, 1974). The problem with this later approach is, as Farr (1969) notes, that the rate factor becomes confounded with the comprehension factor.

Various attempts have been made to avoid this confounding. The principle sometimes adopted has been to include in the text misprinted words or words which completely upset the sense of the sentences. The latter method was used by Tinker (1965, pp. 118–119) for his researches into legibility, although his *Tinker Speed of Reading Test* (Tinker, 1955) is now out of print. These methods have been criticized, for example by Anderson and Dearborn (1952, p. 304), on the grounds that the reader must adopt the attitude of a proof-reader and Tinker himself has warned (1965, pp. 286–7) that speed of reading in one area bears little relationship to speed of reading in another, owing to the variety of materials and the range of purposes for which they are read. Nevertheless, this approach is adopted for measuring the reading speed factor in the most commonly used British test of the English proficiency of overseas students (Davies, 1964).

It might be argued that there is little point in trying to distinguish speed of reading from comprehension since comprehension is essential in silent reading. However, it might also be said that the use of paragraphs followed by questions is unrealistic since the reading is broken up too much, and thus the activity measured is still not normal silent reading. The use of longer passages has also certain disadvantages for, although the task may seem more natural, there are greater difficulties in administration if a measure of rate is being taken. Either the student must be asked to note down the time at which he finishes reading, or he must be made to stop part-way through, as in the one-minute tests. Both approaches are unreliable and the latter has the disadvantage that a reader must read sequentially through the text and cannot, for example, skim through to preview it. Mention must also be made of the technical problem that the questions asked on a passage are not independent items, and that the answers are interdependent. Finally it might be noted that it is difficult to discover what has been gained from a text over what is already known. Tuinman (1974) examined five of the most widely used American standardized tests of reading comprehension and concluded that in none of them was there sufficient guarantee against answering items on the basis of information other than that presented in the passage.

Perhaps it is because of the problems of testing already

mentioned that British tests of silent reading attainment have tended to be of the sentence completion type. Here a sentence or short passage is given with, in brackets, a choice of say four words, one of which must be used to make the best sense of the sentence. The most commonly used British test of silent reading, the *Watts-Vernon* and the *National Survey Form Six* employed in DES surveys of attainment are sentence completion tests. Although the tests themselves are not generally available, there is a useful discussion of them in *The Trend of Reading Standards* (Start and Wells, 1972), which is the report of the latest DES-sponsored national survey of reading standards, and by Davies (1977). The *NFER Reading Test AD* (Watts, 1954) appears to be similar to these cloze tests.

Sentence completion tests have been criticized on a number of grounds, and one forceful comment is from J. C. Daniels (1969), himself a constructor of tests of reading. In the context of the debate over reading standards, he comments that whatever these tests measure (and he suggests it may be vocabulary and comprehension) it is not very close to normal reading. Another criticism may be made in the light of some recent research into cloze procedure (Neville and Pugh, 1976) where it was found that poorer readers encountered proportionately greater difficulty with gaps occurring at the beginning of a sentence than did better readers. The relevance of this finding is that the omitted words in sentence completion tests are normally at, or very near to, the end of a sentence. Hence, it might be argued, the tests may test an even more limited range of reading skill than one might suppose. However, Heaton and Pugh (1975) used an unpublished sentence completion test (Warden, 1956) as one of the measures in attempting to find correlates of academic achievement in a year group of university students from overseas. The sentence completion test was a very good predictor in certain cases and was better than a purpose-made English proficiency test. Of course, one interpretation of this finding is that sentence completion tests measure something very important for study, but that this something is not necessarily reading comprehension.

Cloze tests have been advocated for a number of years as a means of testing comprehension without the disadvantage of comprehension questions. Surprisingly only two standardized cloze tests appear to be available in this country, the *GAP Reading*

Comprehension Test (McLeod and Unwin, 1970) and the *GAPADOL Test* (McLeod and Anderson, 1973). Both of these tests were devised in Australia, but for the *GAP* test British norms are given. Unfortunately the manuals give very sparse information about the reliability and validity of these tests.

Conclusion and summary

The tests referred to so far have been intended mainly for assessing individual or group attainment, although some of them could claim to have a diagnostic function as well. However, the weakness of many tests appears to be that they lack face validity as tests of reading. Few measure an activity akin to fluent reading, for example, and those which are intended to measure reading comprehension appear to be measuring rather different things, none of them obviously close to what a reader does when reading with comprehension.

Of course, any test must take a sample of behaviour, and sampling of mental or intellectual behaviour is difficult. The tests have their uses as measures of standard of attainment when interpreted cautiously. They also have their dangers, however, and in evaluating what is achieved by a course in silent reading, one must be cautious, especially when before and after measures are used. This is because the tests employed will to some extent indicate to both the children or students and to their teachers, what are the aims of a course.

However, as was argued in Chapter 5, there may be no tests available for some of the behaviours which are to be developed. For example, an important aim of a course may be to develop interest in reading and the best means available may well be to keep records of the number of books which children read, or of the time which they spend actually reading during lessons devoted to reading, or in some other way to avoid using a test which, although standardized and reliable, is not measuring what the teacher hopes to develop.

This rather extreme example should not obscure the fact that very few tests are available to measure the aspects of silent reading which it is desirable to teach. A guide, such as that by Heaton (1975), may be useful for teachers to prepare their own tests. Among standardized tests a promising area is the development of tests of reading flexibility (*see* Rankin, 1974 for a review), since these tests are intended to take account of the fact that people read at different rates according to the material they read and the purpose for which they are reading it. In general, however, as in the study of visual behaviour, the testing of reading has taken little account of those aspects of reading behaviour which are most important at the silent stage.

The answer to these problems in measurement is partly to use a range of different measures, ˉ especially in teaching where standardized tests, interviews, observation and questionnaires can be employed. What is clear, however, is that a good deal remains to be discovered not only about testing but about the behaviours which we are trying to test. In this chapter, as elsewhere, stress has been placed on the dangers of over-simple conceptualization based on inadequate or limited techniques for observation and measurement.

Postscript

Two themes have arisen regularly in this book. One is the neglect of the teaching of silent reading and the other is the difficulty of testing and measuring silent reading performance. In fact, it has been seen that the two themes are linked since it is difficult to teach what cannot be easily observed, recorded and assessed. Nevertheless, the importance of the skill of silent reading provides a strong argument for attempting to overcome problems which stand in the way of teaching it. Further experience in teaching silent reading may be necessary *before* testing procedures become more refined, and concern for its teaching is in itself likely to lead to increased activity in the sphere of testing. However, more sophisticated tests which are nevertheless simpler in administration might take some time to develop.

What is to be resisted is the teaching of behaviours whose relevance to realistic reading situations is dubious, but which have gained undue prominence through the apparent ease of testing them. Considerably more thought also needs to be given to what is meant by 'comprehension' and by 'readability' since here, as in the case of speed reading, it appears that measurement devices and the constructs of devisers of tests may sometimes have been misleading for teachers in the classroom.

The field of reading interests, and the broader question of the effect of a text upon the reader, also warrant further investigation. At present we seem to know little of the effect on a child's development of the books he reads, nor do we know much about why he chooses to read certain materials. Nor have the differences been resolved between those whose concern is with literary response and those who are concerned with the more mundane, but also important, question of how best to develop the ability to use books and other writings for obtaining information and for learning.

Fortunately, in view of this listing of what we do not know, there have been signs recently of increased concern, at least among researchers, with reading at this level. Examples from areas mentioned in this book include the renewed interest among psychologists in reading as an information-processing activity, the concern of linguists with longer texts than had hitherto been within their scope, and an emphasis among researchers on observing silent reading under more normal conditions. In teaching silent reading, however, there does not appear to have been much increase in activity, except perhaps in universities, yet it is in schools that silent reading needs to be further developed more urgently than elsewhere. Suggestions have been made here for how this might be done. However, it has been implied that in the long term this may require some radical re-thinking about some major aspects of secondary education. If so, a re-examination seems necessary, since an important purpose of formal education is to equip children for independent learning, for which silent reading is often an essential tool.

References

Alderson, Connie (1968) *Magazines Teenagers Read*. London: Pergamon.

Alexander, J. E. and Filler, R. C. (1977) *Attitudes and Reading*. Newark, Delaware: International Reading Association.

Anderson, A. W. (1969) *Speed up Your Reading*. (Revised edition). Nedlands: University of Western Australia.

Anderson, I. H. (1937) 'Studies in the eye movements of good and poor readers'. *Psychological Monographs*, 215, pp. 21–35.

Anderson, I. H. and Dearborn, W. F. (1952) *The Psychology of Teaching Reading*. New York: Ronald Press.

Ausubel, D. P. (1968) *Educational Psychology: a Cognitive View*. New York: Holt, Rinehart and Winston.

Balfour, A. J. (1888) *The Pleasures of Reading*. Edinburgh: Blackwood.

Barnes, D. *et al.* (1969) *Language, the Learner and the School*. Harmondsworth: Penguin Books.

Barnes, D. *et al.* (1971) 'Group talk and literary response'. *English in Education*, 5(3), pp. 63–76.

Bate, S. M. (1965) *Reading Test EH*. Slough: National Foundation for Educational Research.

Bayley, H. (1957) *Quicker Reading*. London: Pitman.

Bayley, H. (1960) *Speed Up Your Reading*. Manchester: The Carborundum Company.

Beard, Ruth (1972) *Teaching and Learning in Higher Education* (2nd edition). Harmondsworth: Penguin Books.

Berger, A. (1970) *Speed Reading: An Annotated Bibliography*. Newark, Delaware: International Reading Association.

Berger, P. L. and Luckmann, T. (1966) *The Social Construction of Reality*. Harmondsworth: Allen Lane, The Penguin Press.

Binder, Lucia (1976) 'Evaluation of Progress in Spare-Time Reading'. In J. E. Merritt (ed.) *New Horizons in Reading*. Newark, Delaware: International Reading Association, pp. 215–219.

Black, E. L. (1954) *Comprehension Test for College of Education Students*. Slough: National Foundation for Educational Research.

Bloom, B. S. *et al.* (1956) *Taxonomy of Educational Objectives: Handbook 1, Cognitive Domain*. New York: McKay.

Board of Education (1921) *The Teaching of English in England.* (The Newbolt Report). London: HMSO.

Bormuth, J. R. (1968) 'The cloze readability procedure'. *Elementary English*, 45, pp. 429–436.

Bormuth, J. R. (1973) 'Reading literacy: its definition and assessment'. *Reading Research Quarterly*, 9, pp. 7–66.

Brown, J. R., Cramond, J. K. and Wilde, R. J. (1973) 'Children's use of the mass media: a functional approach'. Paper presented to the British Psychological Society Conference (Social Psychology Section), Bristol, September 1973.

Burion, J. (1968) *Axiologie et Méthodologies de la Lecture*, and *La Lecture d'Énonciation et de Compréhension* (vols. 1 and 2 of doctoral thesis). Brussels: Free University of Brussels.

Buros, O. K. (1968) *Reading Tests and Reviews.* Highland Park, New Jersey: Gryphon Press.

Burt, C. (1959) *A Psychological Study of Typography.* Cambridge: Cambridge University Press.

Buswell, G. T. (1920) *An Experimental Study of the Eye-voice Span in Reading.* (Supplementary Educational Monographs, No. 17). Chicago: University of Chicago.

Buswell, G. T. (1945) *Non-Oral Reading: A Study of its Use in the Chicago Public Schools.* (Supplementary Educational Monographs, No. 60). Chicago: University of Chicago.

Buzan, T. (1971) *Speed Reading.* London: Sphere Books.

Buzan, T. (1974) *Use Your Head.* London: BBC Publications.

CACE (1959) *15 to 18.* (The Crowther Report for the Central Advisory Council for Education). London: HMSO.

Calthrop, K. (1971) *Reading Together—An Investigation into the Use of the Class Reader.* London: Heinemann Educational.

Carmichael, L. and Dearborn, W. F. (1948) *Reading and Visual Fatigue.* London: Harrap.

Chambers, A. (1969) *The Reluctant Reader.* London: Pergamon.

Chaytor, H. J. (1945) *From Script to Print: An Introduction to Medieval Vernacular Literature.* Cambridge: Heffer.

Cipolla, C. M. (1969) *Literacy and Development in the West.* Harmondsworth: Penguin Books.

Clymer, T. (1968) 'What is reading?: some current concepts'. In Helen M. Robinson (ed.) *Innovation and Change in Reading Instruction.* Chicago: University of Chicago Press, pp. 7–29.

Conrad, R. (1972) 'Speech and reading'. In J. F. Kavanagh and I. G. Mattingly (eds.) *Language by Ear and by Eye.* Cambridge, Massachusetts: MIT Press, pp. 205–240.

Culhane, P. T. (1976) 'Lexis in Applied Linguistics'. Paper presented to a BAAL Seminar, Nottingham, March 1976. (Reprinted in *Russian*

Language Journal, 31 (109), pp. 25–33, 1977).

Daiches, D. (1956) *Critical Approaches to Literature*. London: Longman.

Daly, B., Neville, Mary H. and Pugh, A. K. (1975) *Reading while Listening: An Annotated Bibliography of Materials and Research*. (Institute of Education Occasional Paper No. 13). Leeds: University of Leeds.

Daniels, J. C. (1969) 'Educational Standards'. In B. Jackson and B. McAlhone (eds.) *Verdict on the Facts*. Cambridge: Advisory Centre for Education, pp. 4–8.

D'Arcy, P. (1973) *Reading for Meaning* (vol. 1 *Learning to Read*; vol. 2 *The Reader's Response*). London: Hutchinson Educational.

Davies, A. (1964) *English Proficiency Test Battery*. London: British Council.

Davies, P. (1977) 'Language skills in sentence-level reading tests'. *Reading*, 11(1). pp. 27–35.

Davies, W. J. F. (1973) *Teaching Reading in England*. London: Pitman.

Davis, F. B. (1944) 'Fundamental factors of comprehension in reading'. *Psychometrika*, 9, pp. 185–197.

Davis, F. B. (1968) 'Research in comprehension in reading.' *Reading Research Quarterly*, 4, pp. 499–545.

Davis, F. B. (1972) 'Psychometric research on comprehension in reading.' *Reading Research Quarterly*, 7, pp. 628–678.

Dearborn, W. F. (1906) 'The psychology of reading'. *Archives of Philosophy, Psychology and Scientific Methods*, 1 (4), pp. 7–132.

Dearborn, W. F. and Anderson, I. H. (1937) 'A new method for teaching phrasing and for increasing the size of reading fixations'. *Psychological Record*, 1, pp. 459–475.

De Leeuw, Manya and de Leeuw, E. (1965) *Read Better, Read Faster: a new approach to effective reading*. Harmondsworth: Penguin Books.

DES (1975) *A Language for Life*. (The Bullock Report for the Department of Education and Science). London: HMSO.

Diack, H. (1964) *Improve Your English: Reading*. London: New English Library.

Ditchburn, R. W. (1973) *Eye-movements and Visual Perception*. Oxford: Clarendon Press.

Dolan, T. and Harrison, C. (1975) *The Incidence and Context of Reading in School*. (Second interim report on the Schools Council Effective Use of Reading Project). Nottingham: University of Nottingham School of Education.

Dudley, G. A. (1964) *Rapid Reading*. Marple, Cheshire: Psychology Publishing Company.

Edfeldt, W. A. (1959) *Silent Speech and Silent Reading*. Stockholm: Almqvist and Wiksell.

Fader, D. N. (1966) *Hooked on Books*. London: Pergamon.

Farnes, N. C. (1973) *Reading Purposes, Comprehension and the Use of Context*.

(Units 3 and 4 of the Open University Reading Development Course no. PE261). Milton Keynes: The Open University Press.

Farr, R. (1969) *Reading: what can be measured?* Newark, Delaware: International Reading Association.

Farr, R. and Weintraub, S. (1975) 'The annual summary—50 years of publication.' *Reading Research Quarterly*, 10, pp. 265–266.

Fawcett, R. (1977) 'Reading Laboratories'. Chapter 7 in E. A. Lunzer and W. K. Gardner (eds.) *The Effective Use of Reading*. (Draft report on a Schools Council Project). Nottingham: University of Nottingham School of Education. (Final report to be published, London: Heinemann Educational, 1979).

Flesch, R. F. (1948) 'A new readability yardstick'. *Journal of Applied Psychology*, 32, pp. 221–233.

Flower, F. D. (1966) *Language and Education*. London: Longmans.

Flower, F. D. (1969) *Reading to learn—an approach to critical reading.* London: BBC Publications.

Francis, R. D., Collins, J. K. and Cassel, A. J. (1973) 'The effect of reading tuition on academic achievement: volunteering and methods of tuition'. *British Journal of Educational Psychology*, 43, pp. 298–300.

Fry, E. (1963a) *Reading Faster: A Manual.* Cambridge: Cambridge University Press.

Fry, E. (1963b) *Reading Faster: A Drill Book.* Cambridge: Cambridge University Press.

Gardner, J. (1966) 'The student reader'. *New Society*, (No. 185), pp. 19–20.

Geyer, T. J. (1972) 'Comprehensive and partial models related to the reading process'. *Reading Research Quarterly*, 7, pp. 541–587.

Gibson, Eleanor J. (1972) 'Reading for some purpose'. In J. E. Kavanagh and I. G. Mattingly (eds.) *Language by Ear and by Eye*. Cambridge, Massachusetts: MIT Press.

Gibson, Eleanor J. and Levin, H. (1975) *The Psychology of Reading.* Cambridge, Massachusetts: MIT Press.

Gilliland, J. (1972) *Readability.* London: University of London Press.

Golinkoff, Roberta M. (1976) 'A comparison of reading comprehension processes in good and poor comprehenders. *Reading Research Quarterly*, 9, pp. 623–659.

Goodman, K. S. (1968) 'Reading: a psycholinguistic guessing game'. *Journal of the Reading Specialist*, 6, pp. 126–135.

Goldstrom, J. M. (1972) *The Social Content of Education 1808–1870: a study of the working-class school reader in England and Ireland.* Shannon: Irish University Press.

Gray, W. S. (1919) 'Principles of method in teaching reading as derived from scientific investigation.' In National Society for the Study of

Education, *Eighteenth Yearbook* (part 2). Bloomington, Illinois: Public School Publishing Company, pp. 26–51.

Gray, W. S. and Rogers, Bernice (1956) *Maturity in Reading*. Chicago: University of Chicago Press.

Greene, H. A., Jorgensen, A. N. and Kelley, V. H. (1942) *Iowa Silent Reading Tests—Advanced*. (Revised edition). New York: Harcourt, Brace and World.

Gregory, R. (1966) *Effective Reading: Tutor's Manual*. Manchester: The Carborundum Company.

Gunning, R. (1952) *The Technique of Clear Writing*. New York: McGraw Hill.

Halliday, M. A. K. and Hasan, Ruqaiya (1976) *Cohesion in English*. London: Longman.

Harris, D. P. (1966) *Reading Improvement Exercises for Students of English as a Second Language*. Englewood Cliffs, New Jersey: Prentice-Hall.

Harrison, C. (1977) 'Assessing the readability of school texts'. Chapter 3 in E. A. Lunzer and W. K. Gardner (eds.) *The Effective Use of Reading*. (Draft report on a Schools Council Project). Nottingham: University of Nottingham School of Education. (Final report to be published, London: Heinemann Educational, 1979).

Haward, L. R. C. (1965) *Reading Comprehension Test for Personnel Selection*. London: Hodder and Stoughton Educational.

Hayes, E. J. (1975) 'The reading habits and interests of adolescents and adults'. In W. Latham (ed.) *The Road to Effective Reading*. London: Ward Lock Educational pp. 148–156.

Hayward, F. Margaret (1971) 'Reading and study instruction in Canadian universities and colleges'. *Journal of Reading*, 15, pp. 27–29.

Haviland, R. M. (1973) *Provision for Adult Illiteracy in England*. Reading: Centre for the Teaching of Reading, University of Reading School of Education.

Heaton, J. B. (1975) *Writing English Language Tests*. London: Longman.

Heaton, J. B. and Pugh, A. K. (1975) 'The relationship between overseas students' English scores and their academic achievement'. *Times Higher Educational Supplement*, No. 178 (14 March 1975), p. 10.

Herber, H. L. (1970) *Teaching Reading in Content Areas*. Englewood Cliffs, New Jersey: Prentice-Hall.

Hittleman, D. R. (1973) 'Seeking a psycholinguistic definition of reading'. *Reading Teacher*, 26, pp. 783–789.

Hodgins, R. C. (1971) 'The text is the adversary'. In G. B. Blaine and C. C. McArthur (eds.) *Emotional Problems of the Student*. (2nd edition). New York: Appleton-Century-Crofts, pp. 207–224.

Hoggart, R. (1957) *The Uses of Literacy*. London: Chatto and Windus.

Holding, D. H. (1965) *Principles of Training*. Oxford: Pergamon.

Holmes, J. A. (1954) 'Factors underlying major reading disabilities at the college level'. *Genetic Psychology Monographs*, 49, pp. 3–95.

Holmes, J. A. and Singer, H. (1966) *Speed and Power of Reading in High School.* (Cooperative Research Monograph, No. 14). Washington: U.S. Government Printing Office.

Huey, E. B. (1908) *The Psychology and Pedagogy of Reading.* New York: Macmillan.

Hurt, J. (1971) *Education in Evolution—Church, State, Society and Popular Education 1800–1870.* London: Rupert Hart-Davis.

Hutchings, M. J. and Hutchings, E. M. J. (1972) *The Edinburgh Reading Tests: Stage 2.* London: University of London Press.

Javal, E. (1879) 'Essai sur la physiologie de la lecture'. *Annales d'Oculistique*, 82, pp. 242–253.

Jenkinson, A. J. (1940) *What do Boys and Girls Read?* London: Methuen.

Jongsma, E. (1971) *The Cloze Procedure as a Teaching Technique.* Newark, Delaware: ERIC CRIER/International Reading Association.

IPC (1975) The Mass Media: *Uses and Gratifications.* (Sociological Monograph No. 11). London: International Publishing Corporation.

Karslake, J. S. (1940) 'The Purdue Eye-Camera: a practical apparatus for studying the attention value of advertisements'. *Journal of Applied Psychology*, 24, pp. 417–440.

Klare, G. R. (1963) *The Measurement of Readability.* Ames, Iowa: Iowa State University Press.

Klare, G. R. (1968) 'The role of word frequency in reading ability'. *Elementary English*, 45, pp. 12–22.

Klare, G. R. (1974) 'Assessing readability'. *Reading Research Quarterly*, 10, pp. 62–102.

Klare, G. R. and Macdonald-Ross, M. (1976) 'Selecting text-books: some preliminary thoughts'. In J. E. Merritt (ed.) *New Horizons in Reading.* Newark, Delaware: International Reading Association, pp. 318–330.

Kolers, P. A. (1968) Introduction to a facsimile reprint of E. B. Huey's *The Psychology and Pedagogy of Reading.* Cambridge, Massachusetts: The MIT Press.

Latham, W. (1975) 'The teaching of reading—a crisis?' In W. Latham (ed.) *The Road to Effective Reading.* London: Ward Lock Educational, pp. 8–16.

Leedy, P. D. (1956) *Improve Your Reading: A Guide to Greater Speed, Understanding and Enjoyment.* New York: McGraw-Hill.

Lunzer, E. A. (1976) 'The effective use of reading'. In A. Cashdan (ed.) *The Content of Reading.* London: Ward Lock Educational.

Lunzer, E. A., Waite, M. and Dolan, T. (1977) 'Comprehension and comprehension tests'. Chapter 2 in E. A. Lunzer and W. K. Gardner (eds.) *The Effective Use of Reading*. (Draft Report on a Schools Council Project). Nottingham: University of Nottingham School of Education. (Final report to be published, London: Heinemann Educational, 1979).

McCall, W. A. and Crabbs, Lelah M. (1925) *Standard Test Lessons in Reading*. New York: Columbia University Teachers College.

McLeod, J. and Anderson, J. (1973) *GAPADOL Reading Comprehension Test*. London: Heinemann Educational.

McLeod, J. and Unwin, D. (1970) *GAP Reading Comprehension Test*. London: Heinemann Educational.

McLuhan, M. (1967) *The Gutenberg Galaxy*. London: Routledge and Kegan Paul.

MacMillan, M. (1965) *Efficiency in Reading*. (English-Teaching Information Centre Occasional Paper, No. 6). London: The British Council.

McNally, J. and Murray, W. (1962) *Key Words to Literacy*. (Curriculum Studies No. 3) London: Schoolmaster Publishing Company.

McQuail, D. (1969) *Towards a Sociology of Mass Communications*. London: Collier-Macmillan.

Mann, P. (1973) *Books and Students*. London: National Book League.

Marchbanks, Gabrielle and Levin, H. (1965) 'Cues by which children recognise words'. *Journal of Educational Psychology*, 56, pp. 57–61.

Mares, C. (1964) *The Way to Effective Reading*. London: English Universities Press.

Mathews, M. M. (1966) *Teaching to Read—historically considered*. Chicago: University of Chicago Press.

Mathieson, Margaret (1975) *The Preachers of Culture*. London: Allen and Unwin.

Maxwell, J. (1977) *Reading Progress from 8 to 15*. Windsor: National Foundation for Educational Research.

Maxwell, Martha J. (1971) 'Evaluating college reading and study skills programs'. *Journal of Reading*, 15, pp. 214–221.

Merritt, J. E. (1970) 'The intermediate skills'. In W. K. Gardner (ed.) *Reading Skills*. London: Ward Lock Educational.

Miller, L. L. (1972) *Teaching Efficient Reading Skills*. Minneapolis: Burgess Publishing Company.

Monty, R. A. (1975) 'An advanced eye-movement measuring and recording system'. *American Psychologist*, 30, pp. 331–335.

Morris, Joyce M. (1966) *Standards and Progress in Reading*. Slough: National Foundation for Educational Research.

Morris, R. (1963) *Success and Failure in Learning to Read*. London: Oldbourne. (New edition, 1973. Harmondsworth: Penguin).

Mosenthal, P. (1976) 'Psycholinguistic properties of aural and visual comprehension as determined by children's abilities to comprehend syllogisms'. *Reading Research Quarterly*, 12, pp. 55–92.

Murphy, R. T. (1975) 'Assessment of adult reading competence'. In D. M. Nielsen and H. F. Hjelm (eds.) *Reading and Career Education.* Newark, Delaware: International Reading Association, pp. 50–61.

Narayanaswamy, K. R. (1973) *Reading Comprehension at College Level.* (CIEFL Monograph No. 8). Madras: Oxford University Press.

Neale, Marie D. (1958) *Neale Analysis of Reading Ability.* London: Macmillan.

Nelson, M. J., Denny, E. and Brown, J. (1960) *Nelson-Denny Reading Test. Vocabulary-Comprehension-Rate.* (Revised edition). Boston, Massachusetts: Houghton Mifflin.

Neville, Mary H. (1975) 'The effect of rate of an aural message on listening and on reading while listening'. *Educational Research,* 18, pp. 37–43.

Neville, Mary H. and Pugh, A. K. (1974) 'Context in reading and listening: a comparison of children's errors in cloze tests'. *British Journal of Educational Psychology,* 44, pp. 224–232-

Neville, Mary H. and Pugh, A. K. (1975a) 'An exploratory study of the application of time-compressed and time-expanded speech in the development of the English reading proficiency of foreign students'. *English Language Teaching Journal,* 29, pp. 320–329.

Neville, Mary H. and Pugh, A. K. (1975b) 'An empirical study of the reading while listening method'. In D. Moyle (ed.) *Reading: What of the Future?* London: Ward Lock Educational. pp. 95–106.

Neville, Mary H. and Pugh, A. K. (1975c) 'Reading ability and ability to use a book—a study of middle school children'. *Reading,* 9(3), pp. 23–31.

Neville, Mary H. and Pugh, A. K. (1976) 'Context in reading and listening: variations in approach to cloze tests'. *Reading Research Quarterly,* 12, pp. 13–31.

Neville, Mary H. and Pugh, A. K. (1977) 'Ability to use a book: the effect of teaching'. *Reading,* 11(3) pp. 13–22.

Neville, Mary H. and Pugh, A. K. (1978) 'Reading while listening: the value of teacher involvement'. *English Language Teaching Journal,* 32(4), (forthcoming, 1978).

Noble, G. (1975) *Children in front of the Small Screen.* London: Constable.

O'Brien, J. A. (1921) *Silent Reading.* New York. Macmillan.

Orwell, G. (1940) 'Boys' Weeklies'. Reprinted in *Selected Essays* (1957). Harmondsworth: Penguin.

Ott, E. (1970) *Optimales Lesen.* Stuttgart: Deutsche Verlags-Anstalt.

Perry, W. G. (1959) 'Students' uses and misuses of reading skills'. *Harvard Educational Review,* 29, pp. 192–200.

Perry, W. G. and Whitlock, C. P. (1948a) *Harvard University Reading Films, Series Two.* Cambridge, Massachusetts: Harvard University Press.

Perry, W. G. and Whitlock, C. P. (1948b) *Selections for Improving Speed of Comprehension*. Cambridge, Massachusetts: Harvard University Press.

Pitkin, W. (1929) *The Art of Rapid Reading : a guide for people who want to read faster and more accurately*. New York: Grosset and Dunlap.

Poulton, E. C. (1961) 'British courses for adults on effective reading'. *British Journal of Educational Psychology*, 31, pp. 128–137.

Pound, E. (1934) *A B C of Reading*. London: Faber & Faber.

Pritchatt, D. (1971) *Annual Report to the Senate Committee on Reading Efficiency Courses*. Leeds: University of Leeds, (internal report).

Pugh, A. K. (1969) 'Some neglected aspects of reading in the secondary school'. *Reading*, 3(3), pp. 3–10.

Pugh, A. K. (1971) 'Secondary school reading: obstacles to profit and delight'. *Reading*, 5(1), pp. 6–13.

Pugh, A. K. (1973) 'Zur Auswahl von Lesestoffen für Jugendliche in England'. In Lucia Binder (ed.) *Analyse, Interpretation und Kritik des Jugendbüches*. Vienna: International Institute for Children's Literature and Reading Research.

Pugh, A. K. (1974) *The Design and Evaluation of Reading Efficiency Courses*. Unpublished M.Phil. thesis: University of Leeds School of Education.

Pugh, A. K. (1975a) 'The development of silent reading'. In W. Latham (ed). *The Road to Effective Reading*. London: Ward Lock Educational, pp. 110–119.

Pugh, A. K. (1975b) 'Approaches to developing effective adult reading'. Paper given to the Fourth International Congress of the International Association for Applied Linguistics. Stuttgart, August 1975. (Reprinted in *Modern English Journal*, 7, pp. 9–15, 1976).

Pugh, A. K. (1976) 'Implications of problems of language testing for the validity of speed reading courses'. *System*, 4(1), pp. 29–39.

Pugh, A. K. (1977a) 'Reading fluency in middle school children'. In J. Gilliland (ed.) *Reading: Research and Classroom Practice*. London: Ward Lock Educational, pp. 91–98.

Pugh, A. K. (1977b) 'Methods of studying silent reading behaviour'. *Research Intelligence*, 3(1), pp. 42–43.

Pumfrey, P. D. (1976) *Reading: Tests and Assessment Techniques*. London: Hodder and Stoughton Educational.

Quiller-Couch, A. (1920) *On the Art of Reading*. Cambridge: Cambridge University Press.

Raistrick, A. and Jennings, B. (1965) *A History of Lead Mining in the Pennines*. London: Longman.

Rankin, E. F. (1974) *The Measurement of Reading Flexibility*. Newark, Delaware: International Reading Association.

Ransom, Grayce A. (1974) Review of (revised) *Iowa Silent Reading Tests*.

Journal of Reading, 17, p. 397.

Reading Laboratory Inc. (1971) *Read Faster for Better Comprehension*. London: MacGibbon and Kee.

Reid, Jessie F. (1973) 'Students who cannot study'. *University of Edinburgh Bulletin*, 9(11), pp. 1–2.

Richards, I. A. (1924) *Principles of Literary Criticism*. London: Routledge and Kegan Paul.

Richards, I. A. (1929) *Practical Criticism*. London: Routledge and Kegan Paul.

Richards, I. A. (1943) *How to Read a Page*. London: Routledge and Kegan Paul.

Richaudeau, F. and Gauquelin, M. and Françoise (1966) *Méthode de la Lecture Rapide*. Paris: Centre d'Étude et de Promotion de la Lecture.

Robinson, F. P. (1946) *Effective Study*. New York: Harper and Brothers.

Robinson, H. A. (1975) *Teaching Reading and Study Strategies: The Content Areas*. Boston, Massachusetts: Allyn and Bacon.

Romanes, G. T. (1883) *Mental Evolution in Animals*. London: Kegan, Paul, Trench.

Rothkopf, E. Z. and Kaplan, R. (1972) 'Exploration of the effect of density and specificity of instructional objectives on learning from a text'. *Journal of Educational Psychology*, 63(2), pp. 87–92.

Ryan, T. A. (1947) *Work and Effort*. New York: Ronald Press.

Sampson, G. (1925) *English for the English*. Cambridge: Cambridge University Press.

Schale, Florence (1971) 'Measuring degree and rate of visual awareness in rapid reading on television'. Paper presented at the National Reading Conference, Tampa, Florida, December, 1971.

Schonell, F. J. and Schonell, F. E. (1962) *Diagnostic and Attainment Testing*. London: Oliver and Boyd.

Schools Council (1965) *English: a Programme for Research and Development in English Teaching*. (Working Paper No. 3). London: HMSO.

Segers, A. (1962) *La Lecture Silencieuse à l'École Secondaire et à l'Université*. (Documents de Psychotechnique Scolaire, Université Catholique de Louvain; Les Mensurations Psychopédagogiques V). Louvain: Nauwelaerts.

Shaw, P. (1961) 'Reading in college'. In N. B. Henry (ed.) *Development in and through Reading*. (60th Yearbook of the National Society for the Study of Education, part 1). Chicago: University of Chicago.

Shayer, D. (1972) *The Teaching of English in Schools, 1900–1970*. London: Routledge and Kegan Paul.

Singer, H. (1965) 'A developmental model of speed of reading in grades three through six'. *Reading Research Quarterly*, 1, pp. 29–49.

Smith, A. de W. (1976) 'Reading skills—what reading skills?' In J. E.

Merritt (ed.) *New Horizons in Reading*. Newark, Delaware: International Reading Association, pp. 39–48.

Smith, F. (1971) *Understanding Reading: A Psycholinguistic Analysis of Reading and Learning to Read*. New York: Holt, Rinehart and Winston.

Smith, F. (1973) *Psycholinguistics and Reading*. New York: Holt, Rinehart and Winston.

Smith, Helen K. (1972) 'Reading for different purposes'. In Vera Southgate (ed.) *Literacy at all Levels*. London: Ward Lock Educational, pp. 89–95.

Smith, Nila B. (1925) *One Hundred Ways of Teaching Silent Reading*. Yonkers-on-Hudson, New York: World Book Company.

Sokolov, A. N. (1960) 'Silent speech in the study of foreign languages'. *Voprosy Psichologii*, 5, pp. 57–64. (Reprinted in *Soviet Education*, 3(7) May 1961, pp. 10–14).

Sokolov, A. N. (1968) *Inner Speech and Thought*. Moscow: Presveshchenie Press. (Translated G. T. Onischenko, New York: Plenum Press, 1972).

Spache, G. D. (1962) 'Is this a breakthrough in reading?' *Reading Teacher*, 15, pp. 258–263.

Spearritt, D. (1972) 'Identification of subskills of reading comprehension by maximum likelihood factor analysis'. *Reading Research Quarterly*, 8, pp. 92–111.

Spencer, H. (1969) *The Visible Word*. (2nd edition). London: Lund Humphries.

Start, K. B. and Wells, B. K. (1972) *The Trend of Reading Standards*. Windsor: National Foundation for Educational Research.

Steinacher, R. (1971) 'Reading flexibility: dilemma and solution'. *Journal of Reading*, 15, pp. 143–150.

Stokes, A. (1978) 'The reliability of readability formulae'. *Journal of Research in Reading*, 1(1), pp. 21–34.

Sutherland, G. (1973) *Matthew Arnold on Education*. Harmondsworth: Penguin Books.

Taylor, W. L. (1953) 'Cloze procedure: a new tool for measuring readability'. *Journalism Quarterly*, 30, pp. 415–433.

Thomas, L. and Augstein, E. Sheila (1973) *Developing Your Own Reading*. (Unit 7 of the Open University Reading Development Course No. PE261). Milton Keynes: Open University Press.

Thomas, L., Augstein, E. Sheila and Farnes, N. (1975) 'Reading-for-learning: the anatomy of a research project'. In W. Latham (ed.) *The Road to Effective Reading*. London: Ward Lock Educational, pp. 171–183.

Thomas, L. and Harri-Augstein, E. Sheila (1976) *The Self-Organised Learner and the Printed Word*. (A report to the Social Science Research Council). Uxbridge: Brunel University Centre for the Study of

Human Learning.

Thorndike, E. L. (1932) *A Teacher's Work Book of 20,000 Words*. New York: Columbia University Teacher's College.

Thorndike, R. L. (1973) ' "Reading as reasoning" '. *Reading Research Quarterly*, 9, pp. 135–147.

Tinker, M. A. (1955) *Tinker Speed of Reading Test*. (Revised edition). Minneapolis: University of Minnesota Press.

Tinker, M. A. (1965) *Bases for Effective Reading*. Minneapolis: University of Minnesota Press.

Tuinman, J. J. (1974) 'Determining the passage dependency of comprehension questions in five major tests'. *Reading Research Quarterly*, 9, pp. 206–223.

Vernon, Magdalen D. (1931) *The Experimental Study of Reading*. Cambridge: Cambridge University Press.

Vernon, Magdalen D. (1969) Review of G. R. Wainwright's *Towards Efficiency in Reading*. *Reading*, 3(2), pp. 33–34.

Vernon, P. E. (1962) 'The determinants of reading comprehension'. *Educational and Psychological Measurement*, 22, pp. 269–286.

Vernon, P. E. (1964) *Personality Assessment*. London: Methuen.

Wainwright, G. R. (1965) *Results of Reading Efficiency Courses held at Hull College of Technology*. Kingston-upon-Hull: College of Technology (internal report).

Wainwright, G. R. (1967) 'Effective training in efficient reading'. *The Technical Journal*, 65(4), pp. 39–40.

Wainwright, G. R. (1968) *Towards Efficiency in Reading*. Cambridge: Cambridge University Press.

Wainwright, G. R. (1969) 'How to halve your reading time'. *The Supervisor*, 20, pp. 104–105.

Waldman, J. (1958) *Rapid Reading Made Simple*. New York: Doubleday and Company.

Walker, L. (1976) 'Comprehending writing and spontaneous speech'. *Reading Research Quarterly*, 11, pp. 144–167.

Warden, V. B. (1956) *Construction and Standardisation of a Reading Comprehension Test*. Unpublished M.A. thesis: University of London Institute of Education.

Watts, A. F. (1944) *Thz Language and Mental Development of Children*. London: Harrap.

Watts, A. F. (1954) *Reading Test AD*. Slough: National Foundation for Educational Research.

Watts, L. and Nisbet, J. (1974) *Legibility in Children's Books*. Windsor: National Foundation for Educational Research.

Watts, W. J. (1969) *Reading Skills: a Critical Look at Dynamic Reading*. Falmer: University of Sussex Centre for Educational Technology.

Watts, W. J. (1972) *A Critical Investigation of Advanced Learning Methods as taught by the College of Advanced Reading.* Falmer: University of Sussex Centre for Educational Technology.

Watts, W. J. and Buzan, A. (1973) 'Reading to learn: a project on advanced learning methods.' *British Journal of Educational Technology,* 2, pp. 132–141.

Webb, R. K. (1958) 'The Victorian reading public'. In B. Ford (ed.) *From Dickens to Hardy.* (Pelican Guide to English Literature, vol. 6). Harmondsworth: Penguin Books, pp. 205–226.

Weber, J. and Schatte, J. (1972) *Lesetraining: eine Anleitung zum Schnelleren Lesen und Besseren Lernen.* Frankfurt-am-Main: Fischer Taschenbuch Verlag.

Webster, O. (1964) *Read Well and Remember.* London: Hutchinson.

Weintraub, S. (1972) *Auditory Perception and Deafness.* Newark, Delaware: ERIC CRIER/International Reading Association.

Wellens, J. (1966) 'Effective Reading: the development of a new training package'. *Industrial Training International,* 1, pp. 111–113.

West, M. (1926) *Bilingualism.* (Bureau of Education, India, Occasional Report No. 13). Calcutta: Government of India, Central Publications Branch.

West, M. (1927) *The Construction of Reading Material for Reading a Foreign Language.* London: Oxford University Press.

Whalley, P. C. and Fleming, R. W. (1975) 'An experiment with a simple recorder of reading behaviour'. *Programmed Learning and Educational Technology,* 12, pp. 120–123.

Whalley, P. C. (1976) Unpublished contribution on observing and measuring reading behaviour to an Institute of Educational Technology Textual Research Seminar, The Open University, 27th February 1976.

Which (1968) 'Rapid reading courses'. pp. 156–160.

Whitehead, F., Capey, A. C. and Maddren, Wendy (1975) *Children's Reading Interests.* (Interim report on Schools Council Project into Children's Reading Habits, 10–15). London: Evans and Methuen Educational.

Wilkinson, A. (1969) 'Research in listening comprehension'. *Educational Research,* 12, pp. 140–144.

Williams, R. (1958) *Culture and Society, 1780–1950.* London: Chatto and Windus.

Wilson, J. (1972) *Philosophy and Educational Research.* Windsor: National Foundation for Educational Research.

Wiomont, B. (1960) *La Lecture Silenciense à l'École Primaire.* (Documents de Psychotechnique Scolaire, Université Catholique de Louvain; Les Mensurations Psychopédagogiques IV). Louvain: Nauwelaerts.

Wiseman, S. and Wrigley, J. (1959) *Manchester Reading Comprehension Test (Senior) I.* London: University of London Press.

Witty, P. (1953) *How to Become a Better Reader*. Chicago: Science Research Associates.

Wood, D. N. (1971) 'And how fast can you read?' *Books for Your Children*, 6(2), p. 12.

Wyndham, J. (1951) *The Day of the Triffids*. London: Michael Joseph.

Yarbus, A. L. (1967) *Eye Movements and Vision*. (Translated B. Haigh). New York: Plenum Press.

Yarlott, G. and Harpin, W. S. (1971) '1,000 responses to English literature (2)'. *Educational Research*, 13(2), pp. 87–91. (Part 1 of this article appeared in vol. 13, no. 1, 1970, pp. 3–11.)

Yorkey, R. C. (1970) *Study Skills for Students of English as a Foreign Language*. New York: McGraw-Hill.

Young, L. R. and Sheena, D. (1975) 'Eye-movement measurement techniques'. *American Psychologist*, 30, pp. 315–330.

Zielke, W. (1965) *Schneller Lesen, Besser Lesen*. Munich: Verlag Moderne Industrie.

Appendix—Reading Laboratories available in Britain

Reading laboratories are boxes containing series of graded cards for children to read and to answer questions on. An essential feature is that children should work at their own pace and keep their own records of progress. The term 'reading laboratory' seems to have been first used in the 1950s by Science Research Associates of Chicago. This company's materials were the first of their kind to become available in this country, but three other publishers now market somewhat similar materials in Britain. It will be noted, however, that it is SRA who have concentrated on the secondary age range.

Drake Educational Associates, 212 Whitchurch Road, Cardiff CF4 3XF publish *Language Centre 1*, for 5–7 year old children and *Language Centre 2* for 7–9 year olds. Each 'language centre' consists of a box containing graded reading cards, answer cards, and cassettes. This scheme is intended to develop not only reading, but other language skills also. There is a 'Teacher's Handbook' and a 'Pupil Log Book' in which children record their progress. In an apparent attempt to overcome some criticisms of laboratory-type materials, each card contains suggestions for further activities and the questions require more substantial answers than is usual.

Longman, Burnt Mill, Harlow, Essex CM20 2JE publish *Reading Routes* for children from 7 to 12 +. This scheme is in a box containing reading cards graded in twelve levels of difficulty, answer cards, a 'Teacher's Guide' and 'My Workbook and Target' in which children write their answers and record their progress.

Science Research Associates, Newtown Road, Henley-on-Thames, Oxfordshire RG9 1EW publish six reading laboratories (reference numbers 2a, 2b, 2c, 3a, 3b and 4a) covering in all the 9–18 age range. Each laboratory contains 'Power Builders' (cards for reading with questions on the text and with exercises on aspects of language such as prefixes, synonyms and definitions). The laboratories also include 'Rate Builders', 'Listening Skill Builders' and answer cards for self-marking: they are accompanied by a 'Teacher's Handbook' and 'Student Record Book'. The purpose is to develop reading, including speed of reading, and listening skills. Laboratories 3b and 4a include practice in note-taking. In addition to reading laboratories, SRA produce a *Reading for Understanding* series. This is also for ages 9–18 and is intended to develop ability to follow a sequence of ideas and draw logical conclusions in reading. The *Researchlab*, for which the age range is not precisely specified, gives practice in locating information in libraries and in various kinds of reference books.

Ward Lock Educational, 116 Baker Street, London WIM 2BB publish the Reading Workshop series. Three 'workshops' are available, for 6–10 year-olds, for 9–13 year-olds, and for remedial work with children from 10 to 14 years. Each workshop comes in a box containing work cards (which provide reading material and questions), answer cards, and a teacher's manual. The pupils have a workbook for recording their answers and progress.

Index of Subjects

Index of Names